3 WKS   821.008 ALL

KT-426-495 ➤

THE NATION'S
FAVOURITE
POEMS OF JOURNEYS

City and Islington Sixth Form College
283-309 Goswell Road
London
EC1
020 7520 0601

CITY AND ISLINGTON
COLLEGE

This book is due for return on or before the date last stamped below.
You may renew by telephone. Please quote the Barcode No.
May not be renewed if required by another reader.

Fine: 5p per day

− 2 DEC 2005

SA013657

Also available from BBC Worldwide:

The Nation's Favourite Poems
ISBN: 0 563 38782 3
ISBN: 0 563 38487 5 (hardback gift edition)

The Nation's Favourite Love Poems
ISBN: 0 563 38378 X
ISBN: 0 563 38432 8 (hardback gift edition)

The Nation's Favourite Comic Poems
ISBN: 0 563 38451 4

The Nation's Favourite Twentieth Century Poems
ISBN: 0 563 55143 7

The Nation's Favourite Shakespeare
ISBN: 0 563 55142 9

The Nation's Favourite Poems of Childhood
ISBN: 0 563 55184 4

Audio cassettes available from BBC Radio Collection:

The Nation's Favourite Poems
ISBN: 0 563 38987 7

The Nation's Favourite Love Poems
ISBN: 0 563 38279 1

The Nation's Favourite Comic Poems
ISBN: 0 563 55850 4

The Nation's Favourite Shakespeare
ISBN: 0 563 55331 6

The Nation's Favourite Lakeland Poems
ISBN: 0 563 55293 X

The Nation's Favourite Poems of Childhood
ISBN: 0 563 47727 X

The above titles are also available on CD

SA013657

THE NATION'S FAVOURITE POEMS OF JOURNEYS

— ◇ —

FOREWORD BY
BENEDICT ALLEN

Published by
BBC Worldwide Limited,
Woodlands,
80 Wood Lane,
London
W12 0TT

First published 2000
Edited and compiled by Alex Warwick
Compilation © BBC Worldwide 2000
Poems © individual copyright holders

All rights reserved. No part of this publication
may be reproduced, stored in a retrieval system,
or transmitted, in any form or by any means,
electronic, mechanical, photocopying, recording or otherwise,
without the permission of BBC Worldwide Limited.

ISBN: 0 563 53715 9

Set in Stempel Garamond by Keystroke,
Jacaranda Lodge, Wolverhampton.
Printed and bound in Great Britain by Martins the Printers Ltd,
Berwick-upon-Tweed.
Cover printed by Belmont Press, Northampton.

LIBRARY

ISLINGTON SIXTH FORM CENTRE

ANNETTE ROAD

LONDON N7 6EX

CONTENTS

— ◇ —

– Contents –

*'Reaching no absolute, in which to rest,
One is always nearer by not keeping still.'*

*'Much have I seen and known; cities of men
And manners, climates, councils, governments,'*

– Contents –

'I travelled among unknown men,
In lands beyond the sea;'

'Who knows what could become of you where
No one has understood the place with names?'

'And as the twilight nets the plunging sun
My heart's keel slides to rest among the meadows.'

– Contents –

'Whose dream is this, I would like to know:
is this a manufactured
hallucination,'

'And I rose
In rainy autumn
And walked abroad in a shower of all my days.'

'Then am I ready, like a palmer fit,
To tread those blest paths which before I writ.'

– Contents –

FOREWORD BY BENEDICT ALLEN

— ◇ —

Journeying is something we all do. It's part of what makes us human. We journey if not by ship or on foot, then in our minds where we may wander free, regardless of whether we are cooped up in a bedsit or spread idly on a summer lawn.

The Nation's Favourite Poems of Journeys, therefore, is not only a glorious collection of travels, but a celebration of an aspect of our nature. As we grow up, and as we live our lives, we share the encounters and departures experienced by the traveller; we know of the gain and loss felt along the way. In short, the tales to be found here are not so much about the arduous treks undertaken by pith-helmeted Victorians, perhaps busily questing after the source of the Nile, as tales of simply being human. That said, among these pages are words powerful enough to carry us as far from our everyday lives as anything found in the tropics. Who is not, just for a moment, stilled by Langston Hughes's evocation of 'ancient, dusky rivers' as they wind slowly on by, each as 'ancient as the world and older than the flow of human blood in human veins'? And who, reading Shelley's 'Ozymandias' isn't suddenly there alongside his explorer in the desert, feeling the level sand underfoot, the taste of dry air as he chances on a great ruler's statue lying shattered and half lost to the wasteland? 'Look on my works, ye Mighty, and despair!' the pedestal's inscription runs, these vain, grandiose words now ridiculed by the greater potency of nature, the dead weight of eternity. 'Nothing beside remains.'

Here then is a book of journeys, each a voyage from the familiar into the beyond. Some poems take us to the equator, some in small circles, some through the dawn, some through darkness and into light. And one, Dylan Thomas's 'Do Not Go Gentle into That Good Night', is a rallying cry to those about to take the final, one-way trip into the afterlife – that might be to nowhere at all.

For someone like me, who has spent twenty years seeking the furthest corners of the globe, it's no surprise that I'm enchanted by the journeys here. But whether you spend your time venturing far afield, or are more armchair bound, it makes little difference. Having read these pages you'll emerge dazed, moved, aroused, stunned, mosquito-ridden. With 'stout Cortez' you'll have stood 'with eagle eyes', the mists licking the tropical forest below, 'silent, upon a peak in Darien.' You'll have been to the furthest reaches of our planet, the furthest shores of the human mind. And the beauty is, your only act of movement will have been to have turned the pages, the words alone will have been your guide to other lands.

'So we must say Goodbye, my darling,
And go, as lovers go, for ever;'

from 'Goodbye'

HENRY CHOLMONDELEY PENNELL 1836–1915

THE NIGHT MAIL NORTH
(Euston Square, 1840)

Now then, take your seats! for Glasgow and the North;
Chester!—Carlisle!—Holyhead,—and the wild Firth of Forth,
    Clap on the steam and sharp's the word,
      You men in scarlet cloth:—

    'Are there any more pas . . sengers,
    For the Night . . Mail . . to the North!'

    Are there any more passengers?
      Yes three—but they can't get in,—
Too late, too late!—How they bellow and knock,
    They might as well try to soften a rock
      As the heart of that fellow in green.

    For the Night Mail North? what ho—
    No use to struggle, you can't get through,
      My young and lusty one—
Whither away from the gorgeous town?—

'For the lake and the stream and the heather brown,
    And the double-barrelled gun!'

    For the Night Mail North, I say?—
      You, with the eager eyes—
You with the haggard face and pale?—

'From a ruined hearth and a starving brood,
    A Crime and a felon's gaol!'

    For the Night Mail North, old man?—
      Old statue of despair—
Why tug and strain at the iron gate?
      'My Daughter!!'

Ha! too late, too late,
She is gone, you may safely swear;
She has given you the slip, d'you hear?
She has left you alone in your wrath,—
And she's off and away, with a glorious start,
To the home of her choice, with the man of her heart,
By the Night Mail North!

. . . . . .

Wh——ish, R——ush,
Wh——ish, R——ush . . .
'What's all that hullabaloo?
Keep fast the gates there—who is this
That insists on bursting through?'
A desperate man whom none may withstand,
For look, there is something clenched in his hand—
Though the bearer is ready to drop—
He waves it wildly to and fro,
And hark! how the crowd are shouting below—

'Back!'—

And back the opposing barriers go,
'A reprieve for the Canongate murderer, Ho!
In the Queen's name-

STOP.'

'Another has confessed the crime.'
Whish—rush—whish—rush. . . .

The Guard has caught the fluttering sheet,

Now forward and northward! fierce and fleet,
Through the mist and the dark and the driving sleet,
As if life and death were in it;
'Tis a splendid race! a race against Time,—
And a thousand to one we win it:

Look at those flitting ghosts—
The white-armed finger-posts—
If we're moving the eighth of an inch, I say,
We're going a mile a minute!
A mile a minute—for life or death—
Away, away! though it catches one's breath,
The man shall not die in his wrath:
The quivering carriages rock and reel—
Hurrah! for the rush of the grinding steel!
The thundering crank, and the mighty wheel!—

Are there any more pas . . sengers
For the Night . . Mail . . to the North?

ANDREW MOTION 1952–

LEAVING BELFAST
For Craig Raine

Driving at dusk on the steep road
north to the airport, *Look back,*
you say, *The finest view of Belfast,*
and point, proud of your choice to stay.

How clear the rows of streetlamps show
which way we came. I trace them slope
by slope through marshlands slipping down
to lanes, and find the roofs again,

their stern geographies of punishment
and love where silence deepens under rain.
Each sudden gust of light explains itself
as flames, but neither they, nor even

bombs redoubled on the hills tonight
can quite include me in their fear.
What does remains invisible, is lost
in curt societies whose deaths become

revenge by morning, and whose homes
are what they pity most.
I watch the moon above them, filling rooms
with cut-out politics, though whether

voices there pronounce me an intruder,
traitor, or a friend, I leave them now
as much a stranger as I came, and my car
beginning on its way again, the road

a hair-line crack, a thread, a wire
I see unwound ahead through miles
of stubborn gorse, until it disappears
at last in darkness, out along the coast.

DOUGLAS DUNN 1942–

A REMOVAL FROM TERRY STREET

On a squeaking cart, they push the usual stuff,
A mattress, bed ends, cups, carpets, chairs,
Four paperback westerns. Two whistling youths
In surplus U.S. Army battle-jackets
Remove their sister's goods. Her husband
Follows, carrying on his shoulders the son
Whose mischief we are glad to see removed,
And pushing, of all things, a lawnmower.
There is no grass in Terry Street. The worms
Come up cracks in concrete yards in moonlight.
That man, I wish him well. I wish him grass.

PHILIP LARKIN 1922–85

POETRY OF DEPARTURES

Sometimes you hear, fifth-hand,
As epitaph:
He chucked up everything
And just cleared off,
And always the voice will sound
Certain you approve
This audacious purifying,
Elemental move.

And they are right, I think.
We all hate home
And having to be there:
I detest my room,
Its specially-chosen junk,
The good books, the good bed,
And my life, in perfect order:
So to hear it said

He walked out on the whole crowd
Leaves me flushed and stirred,
Like *Then she undid her dress*
Or *take that you bastard*;
Surely I can, if he did?
And that helps me stay
Sober and industrious.
But I'd go today,

Yes, swagger the nut-strewn roads,
Crouch in the fo'c'sle
Stubbly with goodness, if
It weren't so artificial,
Such a deliberate step backwards
To create an object:
Books; china; a life
Reprehensibly perfect.

DOUGLAS DUNN 1942–

LEAVING DUNDEE

A small blue window opens in the sky
As thunder rumbles somewhere over Fife.
Eight months of up-and-down – goodbye, goodbye –
Since I sat listening to the wild geese cry
Fanatic flightpaths up autumnal Tay,
Instinctive, mad for home – make way! make way!
Communal feathered scissors, cutting through
The grievous artifice that was my life,
I was alert again, and listening to
That wavering, invisible V-dart
Between two bridges. Now, in a moistened puff,
Flags hang on the château-stacked gables of
A 1980s expense account hotel,
A lost French fantasy, baronial.
From here, through trees, its Frenchness hurts my heart.
It slips into a library of times.
Like an eye on a watch, it looks at me.
And I am going home on Saturday
To my house, to sit at my desk of rhymes
Among familiar things of love, that love me.
Down there, over the green and the railway yards,
Across the broad, rain-misted, subtle Tay,
The road home trickles to a house, a door.
She spoke of what I might do 'afterwards'.
'Go, somewhere else.' I went north to Dundee.
Tomorrow I won't live here any more,
Nor leave alone. *My love, say you'll come with me.*

ALUN LEWIS 1915–44

GOODBYE

So we must say Goodbye, my darling,
And go, as lovers go, for ever;
Tonight remains, to pack and fix on labels
And make an end of lying down together.

I put a final shilling in the gas,
And watch you slip your dress below your knees
And lie so still I hear your rustling comb
Modulate the autumn in the trees.

And all the countless things I shall remember
Lay mummy-cloths of silence round my head;
I fill the carafe with a drink of water;
You say 'We paid a guinea for this bed,'

And then, 'We'll leave some gas, a little warmth
For the next resident, and these dry flowers,'
And turn your face away, afraid to speak
The big word, that Eternity is ours.

Your kisses close my eyes and yet you stare
As though God struck a child with nameless fears;
Perhaps the water glitters and discloses
Time's chalice and its limpid useless tears.

Everything we renounce except our selves;
Selfishness is the last of all to go;
Our sighs are exhalations of the earth,
Our footprints leave a track across the snow.

We made the universe to be our home,
Our nostrils took the wind to be our breath,
Our hearts are massive towers of delight,
We stride across the seven seas of death.

Yet when all's done you'll keep the emerald
I placed upon your finger in the street;
And I will keep the patches that you sewed
On my old battledress tonight, my sweet.

JOHN DONNE 1572–1631

SONG

Sweetest love, I do not go
  For weariness of thee,
Nor in hope the world can show
  A fitter love for me;
    But since that I
Must die at last, 'tis best
To use myself in jest
  Thus by fained deaths to die.

Yesternight the sun went hence,
  And yet is here today,
He hath no desire nor sense,
  Nor half so short a way:
    Then fear not me,
But believe that I shall make
Speedier journeys, since I take
  More wings and spurs than he.

O how feeble is man's power,
  That if good fortune fall,
Cannot add another hour,
  Nor a lost hour recall!
    But come bad chance,
And we join to it our strength,
And we teach it art and length,
  Itself o'er us to advance.

When thou sigh'st, thou sigh'st not wind,
  But sigh'st my soul away,
When thou weep'st, unkindly kind,
  My life's blood doth decay.
    It cannot be
That thou lov'st me, as thou sayst,
If in thine my life thou waste,
  Thou art the best of me.

11

Let not thy divining heart
Forethink me any ill,
Destiny may take thy part,
And may thy fears fulfil.
But think that we
Are but turned aside to sleep;
They who one another keep
Alive, ne'er parted be.

THOMAS HARDY 1840–1928

THE GOING

Why did you give no hint that night
That quickly after the morrow's dawn,
And calmly, as if indifferent quite,
You would close your term here, up and be gone
　　　Where I could not follow
　　　With wing of swallow
To gain one glimpse of you ever anon!

　　　Never to bid good-bye,
　　　Or lip me the softest call,
Or utter a wish for a word, while I
Saw morning harden upon the wall,
　　　Unmoved, unknowing
　　　That your great going
Had place that moment, and altered all.

Why do you make me leave the house
And think for a breath it is you I see
At the end of the alley of bending boughs
Where so often at dusk you used to be;
　　　Till in darkening dankness
　　　The yawning blankness
Of the perspective sickens me!

　　　You were she who abode
　　　By those red-veined rocks far West,
You were the swan-necked one who rode
Along the beetling Beeny Crest,
　　　And, reining nigh me,
　　　Would muse and eye me,
While Life unrolled us its very best.

Why, then, latterly did we not speak,
Did we not think of those days long dead,
And ere your vanishing strive to seek
That time's renewal? We might have said,
       'In this bright spring weather
       We'll visit together
Those places that once we visited.'

       Well, well! All's past amend,
       Unchangeable. It must go.
I seem but a dead man held on end
To sink down soon. . . . O you could not know
       That such swift fleeing
       No soul foreseeing –
Not even I – would undo me so!

COVENTRY PATMORE 1823–96

DEPARTURE

It was not like your great and gracious ways!
Do you, that have nought other to lament,
Never, my Love, repent
Of how, that July afternoon,
You went,
With sudden, unintelligible phrase,
And frightened eye,
Upon your journey of so many days,
Without a single kiss, or a good-bye?
I knew, indeed, that you were parting soon;
And so we sate, within the low sun's rays,
You whispering to me, for your voice was weak,
Your harrowing praise.
Well, it was well,
To hear you such things speak,
And I could tell
What made your eyes a growing gloom of love,
As a warm South-wind sombres a March grove.
And it was like your great and gracious ways
To turn your talk on daily things, my Dear,
Lifting the luminous, pathetic lash
To let the laughter flash,
Whilst I drew near,
Because you spoke so low that I could scarcely hear.
But all at once to leave me at the last,
More at the wonder than the loss aghast,
With huddled, unintelligible phrase,
And frightened eye,
And go your journey of all days
With not one kiss, or a good-bye,
And the only loveless look the look with which you passed:
'Twas all unlike your great and gracious ways.

MICHAEL DRAYTON 1563–1631

SONNET IV

Since there's no help, come let us kiss and part.
   Nay, I have done; you get no more of me,
And I am glad, yea, glad with all my heart,
   That thus so cleanly I myself can free;
Shake hands for ever, cancel all our vows,
   And when we meet at any time again,
Be it not seen in either of our brows
   That we one jot of former love retain.
Now at the last gasp of Love's latest breath,
   When, his pulse failing, Passion speechless lies,
When Faith is kneeling by his bed of death,
   And Innocence is closing up his eyes,
     Now if thou wouldst, when all have given him over,
     From death to life thou mightst him yet recover.

CHRISTINA ROSSETTI 1830–94

REMEMBER

Remember me when I am gone away,
   Gone far away into the silent land;
   When you can no more hold me by the hand,
Nor I half turn to go yet turning stay.
Remember me when no more day by day
   You tell me of our future that you planned:
   Only remember me; you understand
It will be late to counsel then or pray.
Yet if you should forget me for a while
   And afterwards remember, do not grieve:
   For if the darkness and corruption leave
   A vestige of the thoughts that once I had,
Better by far you should forget and smile
   Than that you should remember and be sad.

'*I've topped the wind-swept heights with easy grace,*
Where never lark nor even eagle flew;'

from 'High Flight'

STEPHEN SPENDER 1909–95

THE EXPRESS

After the first powerful plain manifesto
The black statement of pistons, without more fuss
But gliding like a queen, she leaves the station.
Without bowing and with restrained unconcern
She passes the houses which humbly crowd outside,
The gasworks, and at last the heavy page
Of death, printed by gravestones in the cemetery.
Beyond the town there lies the open country
Where, gathering speed, she acquires mystery,
The luminous self-possession of ships on ocean.
It is now she begins to sing – at first quite low
Then loud, and at last with a jazzy madness –
The song of her whistle screaming at curves,
Of deafening tunnels, brakes, innumerable bolts.
And always light, aerial, underneath,
Retreats the elate metre of her wheels.
Steaming through metal landscape on her lines,
She plunges new eras of white happiness,
Where speed throws up strange shapes, broad curves
And parallels clean like the steel of guns.
At last, further than Edinburgh or Rome,
Beyond the crest of the world, she reaches night
Where only a low streamline brightness
Of phosphorus on the tossing hills is white.
Ah, like a comet through flame she moves entranced
Wrapt in her music no bird song, no, nor bough
Breaking with honey buds, shall never equal.

PHILIP LARKIN 1922–85

THE WHITSUN WEDDINGS

That Whitsun, I was late getting away:
   Not till about
One-twenty on the sunlit Saturday
Did my three-quarters-empty train pull out,
All windows down, all cushions hot, all sense
Of being in a hurry gone. We ran
Behind the backs of houses, crossed a street
Of blinding windscreens, smelt the fish-dock; thence
The river's level drifting breadth began,
Where sky and Lincolnshire and water meet.

All afternoon, through the tall heat that slept
   For miles inland,
A slow and stopping curve southwards we kept.
Wide farms went by, short-shadowed cattle, and
Canals with floatings of industrial froth;
A hothouse flashed uniquely: hedges dipped
And rose: and now and then a smell of grass
Displaced the reek of buttoned carriage-cloth
Until the next town, new and nondescript,
Approached with acres of dismantled cars.

At first, I didn't notice what a noise
   The weddings made
Each station that we stopped at: sun destroys
The interest of what's happening in the shade,
And down the long cool platforms whoops and skirls
I took for porters larking with the mails,
And went on reading. Once we started, though,
We passed them, grinning and pomaded, girls
In parodies of fashion, heels and veils,
All posed irresolutely, watching us go,

As if out on the end of an event
   Waving goodbye
To something that survived it. Struck, I leant
More promptly out next time, more curiously,
And saw it all again in different terms:
The fathers with broad belts under their suits
And seamy foreheads; mothers loud and fat;
An uncle shouting smut; and then the perms,
The nylon gloves and jewellery-substitutes,
The lemons, mauves, and olive-ochres that

Marked off the girls unreally from the rest.
   Yes, from cafés
And banquet-halls up yards, and bunting-dressed
Coach-party annexes, the wedding-days
Were coming to an end. All down the line
Fresh couples climbed aboard: the rest stood round;
The last confetti and advice were thrown,
And, as we moved, each face seemed to define
Just what it saw departing: children frowned
At something dull; fathers had never known

Success so huge and wholly farcical;
   The women shared
The secret like a happy funeral;
While girls, gripping their handbags tighter, stared
At a religious wounding. Free at last,
And loaded with the sum of all they saw,
We hurried towards London, shuffling gouts of steam.
Now fields were building-plots, and poplars cast
Long shadows over major roads, and for
Some fifty minutes, that in time would seem

Just long enough to settle hats and say
  I nearly died,
A dozen marriages got under way.
They watched the landscape, sitting side by side
– An Odeon went past, a cooling tower,
And someone running up to bowl – and none
Thought of the others they would never meet
Or how their lives would all contain this hour.
I thought of London spread out in the sun,
Its postal districts packed like squares of wheat:

There we were aimed. And as we raced across
  Bright knots of rail
Past standing Pullmans, walls of blackened moss
Came close, and it was nearly done, this frail
Travelling coincidence; and what it held
Stood ready to be loosed with all the power
That being changed can give. We slowed again,
And as the tightened brakes took hold, there swelled
A sense of falling, like an arrow-shower
Sent out of sight, somewhere becoming rain.

JACKIE KAY 1961–

SASSENACHS

Me and my best pal (well, she was
till a minute ago) are off to London.
First trip on an InterCity alone.
When we got on we were the same
kind of excited – jigging on our seats,
staring at everyone. But then,
I remembered I was to be sophisticated.
So when Jenny starts shouting,
'Look at that, the land's flat already,'
when we are just outside Glasgow
(Motherwell actually) I feel myself flush.
Or even worse, 'Sassenach country.
Wey Hey Hey.' The tartan tammy
sitting proudly on top of her pony;
the tartan scarf swinging like a tail.
The nose pressed to the window.
'England's not so beautiful, is it?'
And we haven't even crossed the border.
And the train's jazzy beat joins her:
Sassenachs sassenachs here we come.
Sassenachs sassenachs Rum Tum Tum.
Sassenachs sassenachs how do you do.
Sassenachs sassenachs we'll get you.
Then she loses momentum, so out come
the egg mayonnaise sandwiches and
the big bottle of bru. 'Ma ma's done us proud,'
says Jenny, digging in, munching loud.
The whole train is an egg and I'm inside it.
I try and remain calm; Jenny starts it again,

Sassenachs sassenachs Rum Tum Tum.
Finally, we get there: London, Euston;
and the very first person on the platform
gets asked – 'Are you a genuine sassenach?'
I want to die, but instead I say, Jenny.
He replies in that English way –
'I beg your pardon,' and Jenny screams
'Did you hear that Voice?'
And we both die laughing, clutching
our stomachs at Euston station.

JOHN MASEFIELD 1878–1967

SEA-FEVER

I must go down to the seas again, to the lonely sea and the sky,
And all I ask is a tall ship and a star to steer her by,
And the wheel's kick and the wind's song and the white sail's shaking,
And a grey mist on the sea's face and a grey dawn breaking.

I must go down to the seas again, for the call of the running tide
Is a wild call and a clear call that may not be denied;
And all I ask is a windy day with the white clouds flying,
And the flung spray and the blown spume, and the sea-gulls crying.

I must go down to the seas again, to the vagrant gypsy life,
To the gull's way and the whale's way where the wind's like a whetted
    knife;
And all I ask is a merry yarn from a laughing fellow-rover,
And quiet sleep and a sweet dream when the long trick's over.

ALLEN TATE 1899–1979

THE MEDITERRANEAN

Quem das finem, rex magne, dolorum?

Where we went in the boat was a long bay
A slingshot wide walled in by towering stone,
Peaked margin of antiquity's delay –
And we went there out of time's monotone:

Where we went in the black hull no light moved
But a gull white-winged along the feckless wave;
The breeze, unseen but fierce as a body loved,
That boat drove onward like a willing slave;

Where we went in the small ship the seaweed
Parted and gave to us the murmuring shore
And we made feast and in our secret need
Devoured the very plates Aeneas bore:

Where derelict you see through the low twilight
The green coast that you thunder-tossed would win
Drop sail, and hastening to drink all night
Eat dish and bowl – to take the sweet land in!

Where we feasted and caroused on the sandless
Pebbles, affecting our day of piracy,
What prophecy of eaten plates could landless
Wanderers fulfil by the ancient sea?

We for that time might taste the famous age
Eternal here yet hidden from our eyes
When lust of power undid its stuffless rage;
They, in a wineskin, bore earth's paradise.

– Let us lie down once more by the breathing side
Of ocean, where our live forefathers sleep
As if the Known Sea still were a month wide –
Atlantis howls but is no longer steep!

What country shall we conquer, what fair land
Unman our conquest and locate our blood?
We've cracked the hemispheres with careless hand:
Now, from the Gates of Hercules we flood

Westward, westward till the barbarous brine
Whelms us to the tired world where tasseling corn,
Fat beans, grapes sweeter than muscadine
Rot on the vine: in that land were we born.

STEVIE SMITH 1902–71

IN MY DREAMS

In my dreams I am always saying goodbye and riding away,
Whither and why I know not nor do I care.
And the parting is sweet and the parting over is sweeter,
And sweetest of all is the night and the rushing air.

In my dreams they are always waving their hands and saying goodbye,
And they give me the stirrup cup and I smile as I drink,
I am glad the journey is set, I am glad I am going,
I am glad, I am glad, that my friends don't know what I think.

RUDYARD KIPLING 1865–1936

MANDALAY

By the old Moulmein Pagoda, lookin' lazy at the sea,
There's a Burma girl a-settin', and I know she thinks o' me;
For the wind is in the palm-trees, and the temple-bells they say:
'Come you back, you British soldier; come you back to Mandalay!'
　　　Come you back to Mandalay,
　　　Where the old Flotilla lay:
　　　Can't you 'ear their paddles chunkin' from Rangoon to
　　　　Mandalay?
　　　On the road to Mandalay,
　　　Where the flyin'-fishes play,
　　　An' the dawn comes up like thunder outer China 'crost the
　　　　Bay!

'Er petticoat was yaller an' 'er little cap was green,
An' 'er name was Supi-yaw-lat – jes' the same as Theebaw's Queen,
An' I seed her first a-smokin' of a whackin' white cheroot,
An' a-wastin' Christian kisses on an 'eathen idol's foot:
　　　Bloomin' idol made o' mud –
　　　Wot they called the Great Gawd Budd –
　　　Plucky lot she cared for idols when I kissed 'er where she
　　　　stud!
　　　On the road to Mandalay . . .

When the mist was on the rice-fields an' the sun was droppin' slow,
She'd git 'er little banjo an' she'd sing *'Kulla-lo-lo!'*
With 'er arm upon my shoulder an' 'er cheek agin my cheek
We useter watch the steamers an' the *hathis* pilin' teak.
　　　Elephints a-pilin' teak
　　　In the sludgy, squdgy creek,
　　　Where the silence 'ung that 'eavy you was 'arf afraid to
　　　　speak!
　　　On the road to Mandalay . . .

But that's all shove be'ind me – long ago an' fur away,
An' there ain't no 'buses runnin' from the Bank to Mandalay;
An' I'm learnin' 'ere in London what the ten-year soldier tells:
'If you've 'eard the East a-callin', you won't never 'eed naught else.'
    No! you won't 'eed nothin' else
    But them spicy garlic smells,
    An' the sunshine an' the palm-trees an' the tinkly temple-bells;
    On the road to Mandalay . . .

I am sick o' wastin' leather on these gritty pavin'-stones,
An' the blasted English drizzle wakes the fever in my bones;
Tho' I walks with fifty 'ousemaids outer Chelsea to the Strand,
An' they talks a lot o' lovin', but wot do they understand?
    Beefy face an' grubby 'and –
    Law! wot do they understand?
    I've a neater, sweeter maiden in a cleaner, greener land!
    On the road to Mandalay . . .

Ship me somewheres east of Suez, where the best is like the worst,
Where there aren't no Ten Commandments an' a man can raise a thirst;
For the temple-bells are callin', an' it's there that I would be –
By the old Moulmein Pagoda, looking lazy at the sea;
    On the road to Mandalay,
    Where the old Flotilla lay,
    With our sick beneath the awnings when we went to Mandalay!
    O the road to Mandalay,
    Where the flyin'-fishes play,
    An' the dawn comes up like thunder outer China 'crost the Bay!

MICHAEL HAMBURGER 1924–

from VARIATIONS I: TRAVELLING

Mountains, lakes. I have been here before
And on other mountains, wooded
Or rocky, smelling of thyme.
Lakes from whose beds they pulled
The giant catfish, for food,
Larger, deeper lakes that washed up
Dead carp and mussel shells, pearly or pink.
Forests where, after rain,
Salamanders lay, looped the dark moss with gold.
High up, in a glade,
Bells clanged, the cowherd boy
Was carving a pipe.

And I moved on, to learn
One of the million histories,
One weather, one dialect
Of herbs, one habitat
After migration, displacement,
With greedy lore to pounce
On a place and possess it,
With the mind's weapons, words,
While between land and water
Yellow vultures, mewing,
Looped empty air
Once filled with the hundred names
Of the nameless, or swooped
To the rocks, for carrion.

Enough now, of grabbing, holding,
The wars fought for peace,
Great loads of equipment lugged
To the borders of bogland, dumped,
So that empty-handed, empty-minded,
A few stragglers could stagger home.

And my baggage – those tags, the stickers
That brag of a Grand Hotel
Requisitioned for troops, then demolished,
Of a tropical island converted
Into a golf course;
The specimens, photographs, notes –
The heavier it grew, the less it was needed,
The longer it strayed, misdirected,
The less it was missed.

Mountains. A lake.
One of a famous number.
I see these birds, they dip over wavelets,
Looping, martins or swallows,
Their flight is enough.
The lake is enough,
To be here, forgetful,
In a boat, on water.
The famous dead have been here.
They saw and named what I see,
They went and forgot.

I climb a mountainside, soggy.
Then springy with heather.
The clouds are low,
The shaggy sheep have a name,
Old, less old than the breed
Less old than the rock
And I smell hot thyme
That grows in another country,
Through gaps in the Roman wall
A cold wind carries it here,

Through gaps in the mind,
Its fortifications, names:
Name that a Roman gave
To a camp on the moor
Where a sheep's jawbone lies
And buzzards, mewing, loop
Air between woods and water
Long empty of his gods;

Name of the yellow poppy
Drooping, after rain,
Or the flash, golden,
From wings in flight –
Greenfinch or yellowhammer –

Of this mountain, this lake. I move on.

JOHN GILLESPIE MAGEE 1922–41

HIGH FLIGHT

Oh, I have slipped the surly bonds of earth
And danced the skies on laughter-silvered wings;
Sunward I've climbed and joined the tumbling mirth
Of sun-split clouds – and done a hundred things
You have not dreamed of; wheeled and soared and swung
High in the sun-lit silence. Hovering there
I've chased the shouting wind along, and flung
My eager craft through footless halls of air;
Up, up the long, delirious, burning blue
I've topped the wind-swept heights with easy grace,
Where never lark nor even eagle flew;
And while, with silent lifting mind I've trod
The high untrespassed sanctity of space,
Put out my hand, and touched the face of God.

'*Reaching no absolute, in which to rest,*
One is always nearer by not keeping still.'

from 'On the Move'

THOMAS BLACKBURN 1916–77

EN ROUTE

It's strange, I thought, though half now stretches
Behind my back, how this road clutches
To its small grit and measuring stone,
Still more of life as I walk on;
Must all directions be subdued
By the compulsion of the road?

And strange it is, since there's no fences,
I do not take the path which glances
Aside from this, as if one strict
Intention gathered up all fact;
Is it because I'm whittled down
To the sharp stones I journey on?

Once certainly the traveller hurried
Down every path the wind unburied.
Finding, however, each new search
Swung back to the old line of march,
And that through detours I could not
Bypass myself or the road's grit,

Though still a side-lane light discloses,
I would hold back from its green mazes,
Sensing, though light it may reflect,
Once entered it would be blunt fact,
And so a double tax be owed
To the compulsion of the road.

Not that today they do not differ,
Myself and the relentless pressure
Of gravel underneath my feet,
But now I glimpse I half beget,
Step after step, what I walk on,
And know I am the origin

Of so much love and hate which gathers
Round those who with me are wayfarers.
Perhaps when to myself, the dreamer,
I wake, and understand the ardour
In which all burn, more clear I'll know
Who others are, myself also,

Than when it seemed far off, the fever
Which shakes me now. Since doom and glamour
No man can fly from or possess,
By stillness I make good their loss,
And find, upon the edge of winter,
More plain the way, as light grows fainter.

Last night I dreamt the road diminished
To a last stone, and where it perished
I met a child beside a river,
Who asked if I would bear him over.
I knelt then as if asking pardon,
But on my back his little burden

Than the whole world became much greater,
As stepping down into the water
I braced myself to find what could
Sustain my feet when I was dead,
And at long last no debt was owed
Since on my shoulders lay the road.

G.K. CHESTERTON 1874–1936

THE ROLLING ENGLISH ROAD

Before the Roman came to Rye or out to Severn strode,
The rolling English drunkard made the rolling English road.
A reeling road, a rolling road, that rambles round the shire,
And after him the parson ran, the sexton and the squire;
A merry road, a mazy road, and such as we did tread
The night we went to Birmingham by way of Beachy Head.

I knew no harm of Bonaparte and plenty of the Squire,
And for to fight the Frenchman I did not much desire;
But I did bash their baggonets because they came arrayed
To straighten out the crooked road an English drunkard made,
Where you and I went down the lane with ale-mugs in our hands,
The night we went to Glastonbury by way of Goodwin Sands.

His sins they were forgiven him; or why do flowers run
Behind him; and the hedges all strengthening in the sun?
The wild thing went from left to right and knew not which was which,
But the wild rose was above him when they found him in the ditch.
God pardon us, nor harden us; we did not see so clear
The night we went to Bannockburn by way of Brighton Pier.

My friends, we will not go again or ape an ancient rage,
Or stretch the folly of our youth to be the shame of age,
But walk with clearer eyes and ears this path that wandereth,
And see undrugged in evening light the decent inn of death;
For there is good news yet to hear and fine things to be seen
Before we go to Paradise by way of Kensal Green.

JOHN POWELL WARD 1937–

THE A40 WOLVERCOTE ROUNDABOUT AT OXFORD

'O' the ubiquitous, the wheel.
A while if only for a while.
A lawn reflecting orange light.
A helipad whence to depart.

Why is he restless? Moons about,
Disturbs the static April night?
O the ubiquitous prayer-wheel,
The ring of lamp-posts tapering tall.

'Welcome to Scholars' Oxenford'
And watch the town roulette-wheel speed
Its bits of centrifugal thought
Off at all angles to the night

As cars brake to its edge, then yield
To let a prior group roar ahead
Then move themselves, or tucked behind
Swing to an exit out beyond,

An arc of concentrated thought.
He paced a little, sensed them do it,
Sat on a civic bench to watch
Them merge and hesitate, guess which

Split-second move a car would make
So miss some other overtake
Some other. None of them remained
More than an instant in his mind,

Not knowing what each driver bore
Most deeply, fears, obsessions, for
Those shed, like clothes, they dropped away
For one lone vagrant passer-by

Witnessing all their stop-start game.
He only saw them go and come
Lane-dodging, weaving, and the wheel
Their curvings made contain them all

As persons, work to suck them in
To this spun centre with its own
Illuminata, then away
'Stratford, The North', infinity.

LOUIS MACNEICE 1907–63

THE WIPER

Through purblind night the wiper
Reaps a swathe of water
On the screen; we shudder on
   And hardly hold the road,
All we can see a segment
Of blackly shining asphalt
With the wiper moving across it
   Clearing, blurring, clearing.

But what to say of the road?
The monotony of its hardly
Visible camber, the mystery
   Of its invisible margins,
Will these be always with us,
The night being broken only
By lights that pass or meet us
   From others in moving boxes?

Boxes of glass and water
Upholstered, equipped with dials
Professing to tell the distance
   We have gone, the speed we are going,
But never a gauge nor needle
To tell us where we are going
Or when day will come, supposing
   This road exists in daytime.

For now we cannot remember
Where we were when it was not
Night, when it was not raining,
   Before this car moved forward
And the wiper backward and forward
Lighting so little before us
Of a road that, crouching forward,
   We watch move always towards us,

Which through the tiny segment
Cleared and blurred by the wiper
Is sucked in under the axle
    To be spewed behind us and lost
While we, dazzled by darkness,
Haul the black future towards us
Peeling the skin from our hands;
    And yet we hold the road.

SEAMUS HEANEY 1939–

NIGHT DRIVE

The smells of ordinariness
Were new on the night drive through France:
Rain and hay and woods on the air
Made warm draughts in the open car.

Signposts whitened relentlessly.
Montreuil, Abbéville, Beauvais
Were promised, promised, came and went,
Each place granting its name's fulfilment.

A combine groaning its way late
Bled seeds across its work-light.
A forest fire smouldered out.
One by one small cafés shut.

I thought of you continuously
A thousand miles south where Italy
Laid its loin to France on the darkened sphere.
Your ordinariness was renewed there.

MOLLY HOLDEN 1927–81

STOPPING PLACES

The long car journeys to the sea
must have their breaks, not always
in towns where there's no room
to park but at the pavement's edge,
in villages, or by the woods, or in lay-bys
vibrating to the passage of fast cars.
The seat's pushed forward, the boot's lifted,
the greaseproof paper
rustles encouragingly. The children
climb to the ground and posture about,
talk, clamber on gates, eat noisily.
They're herded back, the journey
continues.
       What do you think
they'll remember most of that holiday?
the beach? the stately home?
the hot kerb of the promenade?
No. It will often be those nameless places
where they stopped, perhaps for no more
than minutes. The rank grass
and the dingy robin by the overflowing
bin for waste, the gravel ridged by
numerous wheels and the briared wood
that no one else had bothered
to explore, the long inviting field
down which there wasn't time
to go – these will stick in their memories
when beauty spots evaporate.
Was it worth the expense?
                  but
these are the rewards of travelling.
There must be an end in sight
for the transient stopping places
to be necessary, to be memorable.

ROBERT FROST 1874–1963

STOPPING BY WOODS ON A SNOWY EVENING

Whose woods these are I think I know.
His house is in the village though;
He will not see me stopping here
To watch his woods fill up with snow.

My little horse must think it queer
To stop without a farmhouse near
Between the woods and frozen lake
The darkest evening of the year.

He gives his harness bells a shake
To ask if there is some mistake.
The only other sound's the sweep
Of easy wind and downy flake.

The woods are lovely, dark and deep,
But I have promises to keep,
And miles to go before I sleep,
And miles to go before I sleep.

W.H. AUDEN 1907–73

NIGHT MAIL

I

This is the Night Mail crossing the Border,
Bringing the cheque and the postal order,

Letters for the rich, letters for the poor,
The shop at the corner, the girl next door.

Pulling up Beattock, a steady climb:
The gradient's against her, but she's on time.

Past cotton-grass and moorland boulder,
Shovelling white steam over her shoulder,

Snorting noisily, she passes
Silent miles of wind-bent grasses.

Birds turn their heads as she approaches,
Stare from bushes at her blank-faced coaches.

Sheep-dogs cannot turn her course;
They slumber on with paws across.

In the farm she passes no one wakes,
But a jug in a bedroom gently shakes.

II

Dawn freshens. Her climb is done.
Down towards Glasgow she descends,
Towards the steam tugs yelping down a glade of cranes,
Towards the fields of apparatus, the furnaces
Set on the dark plain like gigantic chessmen.
All Scotland waits for her:
In dark glens, beside pale-green lochs,
Men long for news.

III

Letters of thanks, letters from banks,
Letters of joy from girl and boy,
Receipted bills and invitations
To inspect new stock or to visit relations,
And applications for situations,
And timid lovers' declarations,
And gossip, gossip from all the nations,
News circumstantial, news financial,
Letters with holiday snaps to enlarge in,
Letters with faces scrawled on the margin,
Letters from uncles, cousins and aunts,
Letters to Scotland from the South of France,
Letters of condolence to Highlands and Lowlands,
Written on paper of every hue,
The pink, the violet, the white and the blue,
The chatty, the catty, the boring, the adoring,
The cold and official and the heart's outpouring,
Clever, stupid, short and long,
The typed and the printed and the spelt all wrong.

IV

Thousands are still asleep,
Dreaming of terrifying monsters
Or a friendly tea beside the band in Cranston's or Crawford's:
Asleep in working Glasgow, asleep in well-set Edinburgh,
Asleep in granite Aberdeen,
They continue their dreams,
But shall wake soon and hope for letters,
And none will hear the postman's knock
Without a quickening of the heart.
For who can bear to feel himself forgotten?

JOHN BETJEMAN 1906–84

THE METROPOLITAN RAILWAY
Baker Street Station Buffet

Early Electric! With what radiant hope
   Men formed this many-branched electrolier,
Twisted the flex around the iron rope
   And let the dazzling vacuum globes hang clear,
And then with hearts the rich contrivance fill'd
Of copper, beaten by the Bromsgrove Guild.

Early Electric! Sit you down and see,
   'Mid this fine woodwork and a smell of dinner,
A stained-glass windmill and a pot of tea,
   And sepia views of leafy lanes in PINNER, –
Then visualize, far down the shining lines,
Your parents' homestead set in murmuring pines.

Smoothly from HARROW, passing PRESTON ROAD,
   They saw the last green fields and misty sky,
At NEASDEN watched a workmen's train unload,
   And, with the morning villas sliding by,
They felt so sure on their electric trip
That Youth and Progress were in partnership.

And all that day in murky London Wall
   The thought of RUISLIP kept him warm inside;
At FARRINGDON that lunch hour at a stall
   He bought a dozen plants of London Pride;
While she, in arc-lit Oxford Street adrift,
Soared through the sales by safe hydraulic lift.

Early Electric! Maybe even here
   They met that evening at six-fifteen
Beneath the hearts of this electrolier
   And caught the first non-stop to WILLESDEN GREEN,
Then out and on, through rural RAYNER'S LANE
To autumn-scented Middlesex again.

Cancer has killed him. Heart is killing her.
    The trees are down. An Odeon flashes fire
Where stood their villa by the murmuring fir
    When 'they would for their children's good conspire'.
Of all their loves and hopes on hurrying feet
Thou art the worn memorial, Baker Street.

JAMES LEIGH HUNT 1784–1859

THE NILE

It flows through old hushed Egypt and its sands,
  Like some grave mighty thought threading a dream,
  And times and things, as in that vision, seem
Keeping along it their eternal stands, –
Caves, pillars, pyramids, the shepherd bands
  That roamed through the young world, the glory extreme
  Of high Sesostris, and that southern beam,
The laughing queen that caught the world's great hands.
Then comes a mightier silence, stern and strong,
As of a world left empty of its throng,
  And the void weighs on us; and then we wake,
And hear the fruitful stream lapsing along
  Twixt villages, and think how we shall take
  Our own calm journey on for human sake.

STEPHEN SPENDER 1909–95

THE LANDSCAPE NEAR AN AERODROME

More beautiful and soft than any moth
With burring furred antennae feeling its huge path
Through dusk, the air-liner with shut-off engines
Glides over suburbs and the sleeves set trailing tall
To point the wind. Gently, broadly, she falls
Scarcely disturbing charted currents of air.

Lulled by descent, the travellers across sea
And across feminine land indulging its easy limbs
In miles of softness, now let their eyes trained by watching
Penetrate through dusk the outskirts of this town
Here where industry shows a fraying edge.
Here they may see what is being done.

Beyond the winking masthead light
And the landing-ground, they observe the outposts
Of work: chimneys like lank black fingers
Or figures, frightening and mad: and squat buildings
With their strange air behind trees, like women's faces
Shattered by grief. Here where few houses
Moan with faint light behind their blinds
They remark the unhomely sense of complaint, like a dog
Shut out, and shivering at the foreign moon.

In the last sweep of love, they pass over fields
Behind the aerodrome, where boys play all day
Hacking dead grass: whose cries, like wild birds,
Settle upon the nearest roofs
But soon are hid under the loud city.

Then, as they land, they hear the tolling bell
Reaching across the landscape of hysteria
To where, louder than all those batteries,
And charcoaled towers against that dying sky,
Religion stands, the church blocking the sun.

THOM GUNN 1929–

ON THE MOVE

'Man, you gotta Go.'

The blue jay scuffling in the bushes follows
Some hidden purpose, and the gust of birds
That spurts across the field, the wheeling swallows,
Have nested in the trees and undergrowth.
Seeking their instinct, or their poise, or both,
One moves with an uncertain violence
Under the dust thrown by a baffled sense
Or the dull thunder of approximate words.

On motorcycles, up the road, they come:
Small, black, as flies hanging in heat, the Boys,
Until the distance throws them forth, their hum
Bulges to thunder held by calf and thigh.
In goggles, donned impersonality,
In gleaming jackets trophied with the dust,
They strap in doubt – by hiding it, robust –
And almost hear a meaning in their noise.

Exact conclusion of their hardiness
Has no shape yet, but from known whereabouts
They ride, direction where the tyres press.
They scare a flight of birds across the field:
Much that is natural, to the will must yield.
Men manufacture both machine and soul,
And use what they imperfectly control
To dare a future from the taken routes.

It is a part solution, after all.
One is not necessarily discord
On earth; or damned because, half animal
One lacks direct instinct, because one wakes
Afloat on movement that divides and breaks.
One joins the movement in a valueless world,

Choosing it, till, both hurler and the hurled,
One moves as well, always toward, toward.

A minute holds them, who have come to go:
The self-defined, astride the created will
They burst away; the towns they travel through
Are home for neither bird nor holiness,
For birds and saints complete their purposes.
At worst, one is in motion; and at best,
Reaching no absolute, in which to rest,
One is always nearer by not keeping still.

'Much have I seen and known; cities of men
And manners, climates, councils, governments,'

from 'Ulysses'

WILLIAM WORDSWORTH 1770–1850

I WANDERED LONELY AS A CLOUD

I wandered lonely as a cloud
That floats on high o'er vales and hills,
When all at once I saw a crowd,
A host, of golden daffodils;
Beside the lake, beneath the trees,
Fluttering and dancing in the breeze.

Continuous as the stars that shine
And twinkle on the milky way,
They stretched in never-ending line
Along the margin of a bay:
Ten thousand saw I at a glance,
Tossing their heads in sprightly dance.

The waves beside them danced; but they
Outdid the sparkling waves in glee;
A poet could not but be gay,
In such a jocund company;
I gazed – and gazed – but little thought
What wealth the show to me had brought:

For oft, when on my couch I lie
In vacant or in pensive mood,
They flash upon that inward eye
Which is the bliss of solitude;
And then my heart with pleasure fills,
And dances with the daffodils.

SEAMUS HEANEY 1939–

THE PENINSULA

When you have nothing more to say, just drive
For a day all round the peninsula.
The sky is tall as over a runway,
The land without marks so you will not arrive

But pass through, though always skirting landfall.
At dusk, horizons drink down sea and hill,
The ploughed field swallows the whitewashed gable
And you're in the dark again. Now recall

The glazed foreshore and silhouetted log,
That rock where breakers shredded into rags,
The leggy birds stilted on their own legs,
Islands riding themselves out into the fog

And drive back home, still with nothing to say
Except that now you will uncode all landscapes
By this: things founded clean on their own shapes,
Water and ground in their extremity.

CHARLES TOMLINSON 1927–

THE JOURNEY

The sun had not gone down. The new moon
    Rose alongside us, set out as we did:
Grateful for this bright companionship
    We watched the blade grow sharp against the night
And disappear each time we dipped:
    A sliver of illumination at the crest
Awaited us, a swift interrogation
    Showed us the shapes we drove towards
And lost them to the intervening folds
    As our way descended. It was now
The travelling crescent suddenly began
    To leap from side to side, surprising us
At every fresh appearance, unpredictably
    Caught among the sticks of some right-hand tree
Or sailing left over roof and ridge
    To mock us. I know the explanation
But explanations are less compelling than
    These various returns and the expectancy that can
Never quite foresee the way
    The looked-for will look back at us
Across the deviousness of distances that keep on
    Lapsing and renewing themselves under a leaping moon.

ROBERT FROST 1874–1963

THE ROAD NOT TAKEN

Two roads diverged in a yellow wood,
And sorry I could not travel both
And be one traveller, long I stood
And looked down one as far as I could
To where it bent in the undergrowth;

Then took the other, as just as fair,
And having perhaps the better claim,
Because it was grassy and wanted wear;
Though as for that the passing there
Had worn them really about the same,

And both that morning equally lay
In leaves no step had trodden black.
Oh, I kept the first for another day!
Yet knowing how way leads on to way,
I doubted if I should ever come back.

I shall be telling this with a sigh
Somewhere ages and ages hence:
Two roads diverged in a wood, and I –
I took the one less travelled by,
And that has made all the difference.

ALFRED, LORD TENNYSON 1809–92

ULYSSES

It little profits that an idle king,
By this still hearth, among these barren crags,
Matched with an aged wife, I mete and dole
Unequal laws unto a savage race,
That hoard, and sleep, and feed, and know not me.

I cannot rest from travel: I will drink
Life to the lees: all times I have enjoyed
Greatly, have suffered greatly, both with those
That loved me, and alone; on shore, and when
Through scudding drifts the rainy Hyades
Vext the dim sea: I am become a name;
For always roaming with a hungry heart
Much have I seen and known; cities of men
And manners, climates, councils, governments,
Myself not least, but honoured of them all;
And drunk delight of battle with my peers,
Far on the ringing plains of windy Troy.
I am a part of all that I have met;
Yet all experience is an arch wherethrough
Gleams that untravelled world whose margin fades
For ever and for ever when I move.
How dull it is to pause, to make an end,
To rust unburnished, not to shine in use!
As though to breathe were life! Life piled on life
Were all too little, and of one to me
Little remains: but every hour is saved
From that eternal silence, something more,
A bringer of new things; and vile it were
For some three suns to store and hoard myself,
And this grey spirit yearning in desire
To follow knowledge like a sinking star,
Beyond the utmost bound of human thought.

This is my son, mine own Telemachus,
To whom I leave the sceptre and the isle –
Well-loved of me, discerning to fulfil
This labour, by slow prudence to make mild
A rugged people, and through soft degrees
Subdue them to the useful and the good.
Most blameless is he, centred in the sphere
Of common duties, decent not to fail
In offices of tenderness, and pay
Meet adoration to my household gods,
When I am gone. He works his work, I mine.

There lies the port; the vessel puffs her sail:
There gloom the dark, broad seas. My mariners,
Souls that have toiled, and wrought, and thought with me –
That ever with a frolic welcome took
The thunder and the sunshine, and opposed
Free hearts, free foreheads – you and I are old;
Old age hath yet his honour and his toil;
Death closes all: but something ere the end,
Some work of noble note, may yet be done,
Not unbecoming men that strove with Gods.
The lights begin to twinkle from the rocks:
The long day wanes: the slow moon climbs: the deep
Moans round with many voices. Come, my friends,
'Tis not too late to seek a newer world.
Push off, and sitting well in order smite
The sounding furrows; for my purpose holds
To sail beyond the sunset, and the baths
Of all the western stars, until I die.
It may be that the gulfs will wash us down:
It may be we shall touch the Happy Isles,

And see the great Achilles, whom we knew.
Though much is taken, much abides; and though
We are not now that strength which in old days
Moved earth and heaven; that which we are, we are,
One equal temper of heroic hearts,
Made weak by time and fate, but strong in will
To strive, to seek, to find, and not to yield.

W. H. AUDEN 1907–73

AS I WALKED OUT ONE EVENING

As I walked out one evening,
    Walking down Bristol Street,
The crowds upon the pavement
    Were fields of harvest wheat.

And down by the brimming river
    I heard a lover sing
Under an arch of the railway:
    'Love has no ending.

'I'll love you, dear, I'll love you
    Till China and Africa meet,
And the river jumps over the mountain
    And the salmon sing in the street,

'I'll love you till the ocean
    Is folded and hung up to dry
And the seven stars go squawking
    Like geese about the sky.

'The years shall run like rabbits,
    For in my arms I hold
The Flower of the Ages,
    And the first love of the world.'

But all the clocks in the city
    Began to whirr and chime:
'O let not Time deceive you,
    You cannot conquer Time.

'In the burrows of the Nightmare
    Where Justice naked is,
Time watches from the shadow
    And coughs when you would kiss.

'In headaches and in worry
    Vaguely life leaks away,
And Time will have his fancy
    Tomorrow or today.

'Into many a green valley
    Drifts the appalling snow;
Time breaks the threaded dances
    And the diver's brilliant bow.

'O plunge your hands in water,
    Plunge them in up to the wrist;
Stare, stare in the basin
    And wonder what you've missed.

'The glacier knocks in the cupboard,
    The desert sighs in the bed,
And the crack in the teacup opens
    A lane to the land of the dead.

'Where the beggars raffle the banknotes
    And the Giant is enchanting to Jack,
And the Lily-white Boy is a Roarer,
    And Jill goes down on her back.

'O look, look in the mirror,
  O look in your distress;
Life remains a blessing
  Although you cannot bless.

'O stand, stand at the window
  As the tears scald and start;
You shall love your crooked neighbour
  With your crooked heart.'

It was late, late in the evening,
  The lovers they were gone;
The clocks had ceased their chiming,
  And the deep river ran on.

ALFRED, LORD TENNYSON 1809–92

from THE LOTOS-EATERS

'Courage!' he said, and pointed toward the land,
'This mounting wave will roll us shoreward soon.'
In the afternoon they came unto a land
In which it seemèd always afternoon.
All round the coast the languid air did swoon,
Breathing like one that hath a weary dream.
Full-faced above the valley stood the moon;
And, like a downward smoke, the slender stream
Along the cliff to fall and pause and fall did seem.

A land of streams! some, like a downward smoke,
Slow-dropping veils of thinnest lawn, did go;
And some through wavering lights and shadows broke,
Rolling a slumbrous sheet of foam below.
They saw the gleaming river seaward flow
From the inner land: far off three mountain-tops,
Three silent pinnacles of agèd snow,
Stood sunset-flushed; and, dewed with showery drops,
Up-clomb the shadowy pine above the woven copse.

The charmèd sunset lingered low adown
In the red West; through mountain clefts the dale
Was seen far inland, and the yellow down
Bordered with palm, and many a winding vale
And meadow, set with slender galingale;
A land where all things always seemed the same!
And round about the keel with faces pale,
Dark faces pale against that rosy flame,
The mild-eyed melancholy Lotos-eaters came.

Branches they bore of that enchanted stem,
Laden with flower and fruit, whereof they gave
To each, but whoso did receive of them
And taste, to him the gushing of the wave

Far far away did seem to mourn and rave
On alien shores; and if his fellow spake,
His voice was thin, as voices from the grave;
And deep-asleep he seemed, yet all awake,
And music in his ears his beating heart did make.

They sat them down upon the yellow sand,
Between the sun and moon upon the shore;
And sweet it was to dream of Fatherland,
Of child, and wife, and slave; but evermore
Most weary seemed the sea, weary the oar,
Weary the wandering fields of barren foam.
Then some one said, 'We will return no more;'
And all at once they sang, 'Our island home
Is far beyond the wave; we will no longer roam.'

SAMUEL TAYLOR COLERIDGE 1772–1834

from THE RIME OF THE ANCIENT MARINER

PART THE FIRST

It is an ancient Mariner
And he stoppeth one of three.
'By thy long grey beard and glittering eye,
Now wherefore stopp'st thou me?

The Bridegroom's doors are opened wide,
And I am next of kin;
The guests are met, the feast is set:
May'st hear the merry din.'

He holds him with his skinny hand,
There was a ship, quoth he.
'Hold off! unhand me, grey-beard loon!'
Eftsoons his hand dropt he.

He holds him with his glittering eye –
The Wedding-Guest stood still,
And listens like a three years' child:
The Mariner hath his will.

The Wedding-Guest sat on a stone:
He cannot choose but hear;
And thus spake on that ancient man,
The bright-eyed Mariner.

The ship was cheered, the harbour cleared,
Merrily did we drop
Below the kirk, below the hill,
Below the lighthouse top.

The Sun came up upon the left,
Out of the sea came he!
And he shone bright, and on the right
Went down into the sea.

Higher and higher every day,
Till over the mast at noon –
The Wedding-Guest here beat his breast,
For he heard the loud bassoon.

The bride hath paced into the hall,
Red as a rose is she;
Nodding their heads before her goes
The merry minstrelsy.

The Wedding-Guest he beat his breast,
Yet he cannot choose but hear;
And thus spake on that ancient man,
The bright-eyed Mariner.

And now the storm-blast came, and he
Was tyrannous and strong:
He struck with his o'ertaking wings,
And chased us south along.

With sloping masts and dipping prow,
As who pursued with yell and blow
Still treads the shadow of his foe
And forward bends his head,
The ship drove fast, loud roared the blast,
And southward aye we fled.

And now there came both mist and snow,
And it grew wondrous cold:
And ice, mast-high, came floating by,
As green as emerald.

And through the drifts the snowy clifts
Did send a dismal sheen:
Nor shapes of men nor beasts we ken –
The ice was all between.

The ice was here, the ice was there,
The ice was all around:
It cracked and growled, and roared and howled,
Like noises in a swound!

At length did cross an Albatross:
Through the fog it came;
As if it had been a Christian soul,
We hailed it in God's name.

It ate the food it ne'er had eat,
And round and round it flew.
The ice did split with a thunder-fit;
The helmsman steered us through!

And a good south wind sprung up behind;
The Albatross did follow,
And every day, for food or play,
Came to the mariners' hollo!

In mist or cloud, on mast or shroud,
It perched for vespers nine;
Whiles all the night, through fog-smoke white,
Glimmered the white Moon-shine.

'God save thee, ancient Mariner!
From the fiends, that plague thee thus! –
Why look'st thou so?' – With my crossbow
I shot the Albatross.

WALTER DE LA MARE 1873–1956

SEA-MAGIC
To R.I.

My heart faints in me for the distant sea.
  The roar of London is the roar of ire
  The lion utters in his old desire
For Libya out of dim captivity.

The long bright silver of Cheapside I see,
  Her gilded weathercocks on roof and spire
  Exulting eastward in the western fire;
All things recall one heart-sick memory:–

Ever the rustle of the advancing foam,
  The surges' desolate thunder, and the cry
  As of some lone babe in the whispering sky;
Ever I peer into the restless gloom
  To where a ship clad dim and loftily
Looms steadfast in the wonder of her home.

SYLVIA PLATH 1932–63

CHANNEL CROSSING

On storm-struck deck, wind sirens caterwaul;
With each tilt, shock and shudder, our blunt ship
Cleaves forward into fury; dark as anger,
Waves wallop, assaulting the stubborn hull.
Flayed by spray, we take the challenge up,
Grip the rail, squint ahead, and wonder how much longer

Such force can last; but beyond, the neutral view
Shows, rank on rank, the hungry seas advancing.
Below, rocked havoc-sick, voyagers lie
Retching in bright orange basins; a refugee
Sprawls, hunched in black, among baggage, wincing
Under the strict mask of his agony.

Far from the sweet stench of that perilous air
In which our comrades are betrayed, we freeze
And marvel at the smashing nonchalance
Of nature: what better way to test taut fiber
Than against this onslaught, these casual blasts of ice
That wrestle with us like angels; the mere chance

Of making harbor through this racketing flux
Taunts us to valor. Blue sailors sang that our journey
Would be full of sun, white gulls, and water drenched
With radiance, peacock-colored; instead, bleak rocks
Jutted early to mark our going, while sky
Curded over with clouds and chalk cliffs blanched

In sullen light of the inauspicious day.
Now, free, by hazard's quirk, from the common ill
Knocking our brothers down, we strike a stance
Most mock-heroic, to cloak our waking awe
At this rare rumpus which no man can control:
Meek and proud both fall; stark violence

Lays all walls waste; private estates are torn,
Ransacked in the public eye. We forsake
Our lone luck now, compelled by bond, by blood,
To keep some unsaid pact; perhaps concern
Is helpless here, quite extra, yet we must make
The gesture, bend and hold the prone man's head.

And so we sail toward cities, streets and homes
Of other men, where statues celebrate
Brave acts played out in peace, in war; all dangers
End: green shores appear; we assume our names,
Our luggage, as docks halt our brief epic; no debt
Survives arrival; we walk the plank with strangers.

ANON

———

from THE SEAFARER

I sing my own true story, tell my travels,
How I have often suffered times of hardship
In days of toil, and have experienced
Bitter anxiety, my troubled home
On many a ship has been the heaving waves,
Where grim night-watch has often been my lot
At the ship's prow as it beat past the cliffs.
Oppressed by cold my feet were bound by frost
In icy bonds, while worries simmered hot
About my heart, and hunger from within
Tore the sea-weary spirit. He knows not,
Who lives most easily on land, how I
Have spent my winter on the ice-cold sea,
Wretched and anxious, in the paths of exile,
Lacking dear friends, hung round by icicles,
While hail flew past in showers. There heard I nothing
But the resounding sea, the ice-cold waves.
Sometimes I made the song of the wild swan
My pleasure, or the gannet's call, the cries
Of curlews for the missing mirth of men,
The singing gull instead of mead in hall.
Storms beat the rocky cliffs, and icy-winged
The tern replied, the horn-beaked eagle shrieked.
No patron had I there who might have soothed
My desolate spirit. He can little know
Who, proud and flushed with wine, has spent his time
With all the joys of life among the cities,
Safe from such fearful venturings, how I
Have often suffered weary on the seas.
Night shadows darkened, snow came from the north,
Frost bound the earth and hail fell on the ground,
Coldest of corns. And yet the heart's desires
Incite me now that I myself should go
On towering seas, among the salt waves' play;

And constantly the heartfelt wishes urge
The spirit to venture, that I should go forth
To see the lands of strangers far away.
Yet no man in the world's so proud of heart,
So generous of gifts, so bold in youth,
In deeds so brave, or with so loyal lord,
That he can ever venture on the sea
Without great fears of what the Lord may bring.
His mind dwells not on the harmonious harp,
On ring-receiving, or the joy of woman,
Or wordly hopes, or anything at all
But the relentless rolling of the waves;
But he who goes to sea must ever yearn.
The groves bear blossom, cities grow more bright,
The fields adorn themselves, the world speeds up;
Yet all this urges forth the eager spirit
Of him who then desires to travel far
On the sea-paths. Likewise the cuckoo calls
With boding voice, the harbinger of summer
Offers but bitter sorrow in the breast.
The man who's blest with comfort does not know
What some then suffer who most widely travel
The paths of exile. Even now my heart
Journeys beyond its confines, and my thoughts
Over the sea, across the whale's domain,
Travel afar the regions of the earth,
And then come back to me with greed and longing.
The cuckoo cries, incites the eager breast
On to the whale's roads irresistibly,
Over the wide expanses of the sea,
Because the joys of God mean more to me
Than this dead transitory life on land.
That earthly wealth lasts to eternity
I don't believe. Always one of three things

Keeps all in doubt until one's destined hour.
Sickness, old age, the sword, each one of these
May end the lives of doomed and transient men.
Therefore for every warrior the best
Memorial is the praise of living men
After his death, that ere he must depart
He shall have done good deeds on earth against
The malice of his foes, and noble works
Against the devil, that the sons of men
May after praise him, and his glory live
For ever with the angels in the splendour
Of lasting life, in bliss among those hosts.

LANGSTON HUGHES 1902–67

THE NEGRO SPEAKS OF RIVERS
To W.E.B. Du Bois

I've known rivers:
I've known rivers ancient as the world and older than the
    flow of human blood in human veins.
My soul has grown deep like the rivers.

I bathed in the Euphrates when dawns were young.
I built my hut near the Congo and it lulled me to sleep.
I looked upon the Nile and raised the pyramids above it.
I heard the singing of the Mississippi when Abe Lincoln
    went down to New Orleans, and I've seen its muddy
    bosom turn all golden in the sunset.

I've known rivers:
Ancient, dusky rivers.

My soul has grown deep like the rivers.

'*I travelled among unknown men,*
In lands beyond the sea;'

from 'Lucy'

JOHN MILTON 1608–74

---

from PARADISE LOST

XII
[The Banishment]

So spake our mother Eve, and Adam heard
Well pleased, but answered not; for now too nigh
The Archangel stood, and from the other hill
To their fixed station, all in bright array
The Cherubim descended; on the ground
Gliding metéorous, as evening mist
Risen from a river o'er the marish glides,
And gathers ground fast at the labourer's heel
Homeward returning. High in front advanced,
The brandished sword of God before them blazed
Fierce as a comet; which with torrid heat,
And vapour as the Libyan air adust,
Began to parch that temperate clime; whereat
In either hand the hastening Angel caught
Our lingering parents, and to the eastern gate
Led them direct, and down the cliff as fast
To the subjected plain; then disappeared.
They, looking back, all the eastern side beheld
Of Paradise, so late their happy seat,
Waved over by that flaming brand, the gate
With dreadful faces thronged and fiery arms.
Some natural tears they dropped, but wiped them soon;
The world was all before them, where to choose
Their place of rest, and Providence their guide:
They hand in hand, with wandering steps and slow,
Through Eden took their solitary way.

RUPERT BROOKE 1887–1915

THE SOLDIER

If I should die, think only this of me:
    That there's some corner of a foreign field
That is for ever England. There shall be
    In that rich earth a richer dust concealed;
A dust whom England bore, shaped, made aware,
    Gave, once, her flowers to love, her ways to roam,
A body of England's, breathing English air,
    Washed by the rivers, blest by suns of home.

And think, this heart, all evil shed away,
    A pulse in the eternal mind, no less
        Gives somewhere back the thoughts by England given;
Her sights and sounds; dreams happy as her day;
    And laughter, learnt of friends; and gentleness,
        In hearts at peace, under an English heaven.

WILLIAM SHAKESPEARE 1564–1616

SONNET XCVIII

From you have I been absent in the spring,
    When proud pied April, dressed in all his trim,
Hath put a spirit of youth in every thing,
    That heavy Saturn laughed and leaped with him.
Yet nor the lays of birds, nor the sweet smell
    Of different flowers in odour and in hue,
Could make me any summer's story tell,
    Or from their proud lap pluck them where they grew:
Nor did I wonder at the lily's white,
    Nor praise the deep vermilion in the rose;
They were but sweet, but figures of delight,
    Drawn after you, you pattern of all those.
        Yet seemed it winter still, and, you away,
        As with your shadow I with these did play.

WILLIAM WORDSWORTH 1770–1850

from LUCY

III

I travelled among unknown men,
  In lands beyond the sea;
Nor, England! did I know till then
  What love I bore to thee.

'Tis past, that melancholy dream!
  Nor will I quit thy shore
A second time; for still I seem
  To love thee more and more.

Among thy mountains did I feel
  The joy of my desire;
And she I cherished turned her wheel
  Beside an English fire.

Thy mornings showed, thy nights concealed,
  The bowers where Lucy played;
And thine too is the last green field
  That Lucy's eyes surveyed.

ROBERT BROWNING 1812–89

HOME-THOUGHTS, FROM ABROAD

I

Oh, to be in England
Now that April's there,
And whoever wakes in England
Sees, some morning, unaware,
That the lowest boughs and the brushwood sheaf
Round the elm-tree bole are in tiny leaf,
While the chaffinch sings on the orchard bough
In England – now!

II

And after April, when May follows,
And the whitethroat builds, and all the swallows!
Hark, where my blossomed pear-tree in the hedge
Leans to the field and scatters on the clover
Blossoms and dewdrops – at the bent spray's edge –
That's the wise thrush; he sings each song twice over,
Lest you should think he never could recapture
The first fine careless rapture!
And though the fields look rough with hoary dew
All will be gay when noontide wakes anew
The buttercups, the little children's dower
– Far brighter than this gaudy melon-flower!

ROBERT LOUIS STEVENSON 1850–94

SWALLOWS TRAVEL TO AND FRO

Swallows travel to and fro,
And the great winds come and go,
And the steady breezes blow,
    Bearing perfume, bearing love.
Breezes hasten, swallows fly,
Towered clouds forever ply,
And at noonday you and I
    See the same sun shine above.

Dew and rain fall everywhere,
Harvests ripen, flowers are fair,
And the whole round earth is bare
    To the moonshine and the sun;
And the live air, fanned with wings,
Bright with breeze and sunshine, brings
Into contact distant things,
    And makes all the countries one.

Let us wander where we will,
Something kindred greets us still;
Something seen on vale or hill
    Falls familiar on the heart;
So, at scent or sound or sight,
Severed souls by day and night
Tremble with the same delight –
    Tremble, half the world apart.

GRACE NICHOLS 1950–

WHEREVER I HANG

I leave me people, me land, me home
For reasons, I not too sure
I forsake de sun
And de humming-bird splendour
Had big rats in de floorboard
So I pick up me new-world-self
And come, to this place call England
At first I feeling like I in dream –
De misty greyness
I touching de walls to see if they real
They solid to de seam
And de people pouring from de underground system
Like beans
And when I look up to de sky
I see Lord Nelson high – too high to lie

And is so I sending home photos of myself
Among de pigeons and de snow
And is so I warding off de cold
And is so, little by little
I begin to change my calypso ways
Never visiting nobody
Before giving them clear warning
And waiting me turn in queue
Now, after all this time
I get accustom to de English life
But I still miss back-home side
To tell you de truth
I don't know really where I belaang

Yes, divided to de ocean
Divided to de bone

Wherever I hang me knickers – that's my home.

MERLE COLLINS 1950–

WHERE THE SCATTERING BEGAN

Here, on the streets of London
where, some say, the scattering began
we come to find our faces again
We come to measure the rhythm of our paces
against the call of the Ghanaian drum that talks
against the wail of the mbira from Zimbabwe
that yields music to the thumbs
We come with faces denying names
gone English, Irish, Scottish
We come with hands that speak
in ways the tongue has forgotten
We come with intonations
that reshape languages we have been given
We come with eyes that tell a story
the brain cannot recall
We come with the blue of the sea so close
that we lift our eyes with yearning
to the emptiness of the skies
Some of us come with the memory of
forest sounds that we have never known
We all come speaking so simply
of complicated things. Here
when we recognize each other
on the streets of London
hands and eyes and ears
begin to shape answers
to questions tongue can find
no words for asking.

DEREK WALCOTT 1930–

A FAR CRY FROM AFRICA

A wind is ruffling the tawny pelt
Of Africa. Kikuyu, quick as flies,
Batten upon the bloodstreams of the veldt.
Corpses are scattered through a paradise.
Only the worm, colonel of carrion, cries:
'Waste no compassion on these separate dead!'
Statistics justify and scholars seize
The salients of colonial policy.
What is that to the white child hacked in bed?
To savages, expendable as Jews?

Threshed out by beaters, the long rushes break
In a white dust of ibises whose cries
Have wheeled since civilization's dawn
From the parched river or beast-teeming plain.
The violence of beast on beast is read
As natural law, but upright man
Seeks his divinity by inflicting pain.
Delirious as these worried beasts, his wars
Dance to the tightened carcass of a drum,
While he calls courage still that native dread
Of the white peace contracted by the dead.

Again brutish necessity wipes its hands
Upon the napkin of a dirty cause, again
A waste of our compassion, as with Spain,
The gorilla wrestles with the superman.
I who am poisoned with the blood of both,
Where shall I turn, divided to the vein?
I who have cursed
The drunken officer of British rule, how choose
Between this Africa and the English tongue I love?
Betray them both, or give back what they give?
How can I face such slaughter and be cool?
How can I turn from Africa and live?

GRACE NICHOLS 1950–

OUT OF AFRICA

Out of Africa of the suckling
Out of Africa of the tired woman in earrings
Out of Africa of the black-foot leap
Out of Africa of the baobab, the suck-teeth
Out of Africa of the dry maw of hunger
Out of Africa of the first rains, the first mother.

Into the Caribbean of the staggeringly blue sea-eye
Into the Caribbean of the baleful tourist glare
Into the Caribbean of the hurricane
Into the Caribbean of the flame tree, the palm tree,
the ackee, the high smelling saltfish
and the happy creole so-called mentality.

Into England of the frost and the tea
Into England of the budgie and the strawberry
Into England of the trampled autumn tongues
Into England of the meagre funerals
Into England of the hand of the old woman
And the gent running behind someone
who's forgotten their umbrella, crying out,
'I say . . . I say-ay.'

'Who knows what could become of you where
No one has understood the place with names?'

from 'For a Journey'

MICHAEL DRAYTON 1563–1631

TO THE VIRGINIAN VOYAGE

You brave heroic minds
    Worthy your country's name,
      That honour still pursue;
      Go and subdue!
Whilst loitering hinds
    Lurk here at home with shame.

Britons, you stay too long:
    Quickly aboard bestow you
      And with a merry gale
      Swell your stretched sail
With vows as strong
    As the winds that blow you.

Your course securely steer,
    West and by south forth keep
      Rocks, lee-shores, nor shoals
      When Eolus scowls
You need not fear;
    So absolute the deep.

And cheerfully at sea
    Success you still entice
      To get the pearl and gold,
      And ours to hold
VIRGINIA,
    Earth's only paradise.

Where nature hath in store
    Fowl, venison, and fish,
      And the fruitfullest soil
      Without your toil
Three harvests more,
    All greater than your wish.

And the ambitious vine
　　Crowns with his purple mass
　　　The cedar reaching high
　　　To kiss the sky,
The cypress, pine,
　　And useful sassafras.

To whom the Golden Age
　　Still nature's laws doth give,
　　　No other cares attend,
　　　But them to defend
From winter's rage,
　　That long there doth not live.

When as the luscious smell
　　Of that delicious land
　　　Above the seas that flows
　　　The clear wind throws,
Your hearts to swell
　　Approaching the dear strand;

In kenning of the shore
　　(Thanks to God first given)
　　　O you the happiest men,
　　　Be frolic then!
Let cannons roar,
　　Frighting the wide heaven.

And in regions far,
　　Such heroes bring ye forth
　　　As those from whom we came;
　　　And plant our name
Under that star
　　Not known unto our North.

And as there plenty grows
  Of laurel everywhere –
    Apollo's sacred tree –
    You it may see
A poet's brows
  To crown, that may sing there.

Thy *Voyages* attend,
  Industrious Hakluyt,
    Whose reading shall inflame
    Men to seek fame,
And much commend
  To after times thy wit.

ANDREW MARVELL 1621–78

BERMUDAS

Where the remote Bermudas ride,
In th' ocean's bosom unespied,
From a small boat that rowed along,
The listening winds received this song:
    'What should we do but sing His praise,
That led us through the watery maze
Unto an isle so long unknown,
And yet far kinder than our own?
Where He the huge sea monsters wracks,
That lift the deep upon their backs;
He lands us on a grassy stage,
Safe from the storms, and prelate's rage.
He gave us this eternal spring
Which here enamels everything,
And sends the fowls to us in care,
On daily visits through the air;
He hangs in shades the orange bright,
Like golden lamps in a green night,
And does in the pomegranates close
Jewels more rich than Ormus shows;
He makes the figs our mouths to meet,
And throws the melons at our feet;
But apples plants of such a price,
No tree could ever bear them twice;
With cedars, chosen by His hand,
From Lebanon, He stores the land;
And makes the hollow seas, that roar,
Proclaim the ambergris on shore;
He cast (of which we rather boast)
The Gospel's pearl upon our coast,
And in these rocks for us did frame
A temple, where to sound His name.
O! let our voice His praise exalt,
Till it arrive at heaven's vault,

Which, thence (perhaps) rebounding, may
Echo beyond the Mexique Bay.'
    Thus sung they in the English boat,
An holy and a cheerful note;
And all the way, to guide their chime,
With falling oars they kept the time.

EDWARD KAMAU BRATHWAITE 1930–

from THE ARRIVANTS: A NEW WORLD TRILOGY

NEW WORLD A-COMIN'

1

Helpless like this
leader-
less like this,
heroless,
we met you: lover,
warrior, hater,
coming through the files
of the forest
soft foot
to soft soil
of silence:
we met in the soiled
tunnel of leaves.

Click lock
your fire-
lock fore-
arm fire-
arm flashed
fire and our firm
fleshed, flame
warm, fly
bitten warriors
fell.

How long
how long
O Lord
O devil
O fire
O flame
have we walked

have we journeyed
to this place
to this meeting
this shock
and shame
in the soiled
silence.

How long have we
travelled down
valleys down
slopes, silica
glinted, stones
dry as water,
to this flash
of flame in the forest.
O who now will help
us, help-
less, horse-
less, leader-
less, no
hope, no
Hawkins, no
Cortez to come.
Prempeh imprisoned,
Tawiah dead,
Asantewa bridled
and hung.
O who now can help
us: Geronimo, Tackie,
Montezuma to come.

And the fire, our
fire, fashioning locks,

rocks darker than iron;
fire betrayed us once
in our village; now
in the forest, fire falls
us like birds, hot pods
in our belly. Fire
falls walls, fashions
these fire-
locks darker than iron,
and we filed down the path
linked in a new
clinked silence of iron.

2

It will be a long long time before we see
this land again, these trees
again, drifting inland with the sound
of surf, smoke rising

It will be a long long time before we see
these farms again, soft wet slow green
again: Aburi, Akwamu,
mist rising

Watch now these hard men, cold
clear eye'd like the water we ride,
skilful with sail and the rope and the tackle

Watch now these cold men, bold
as the water banging the bow in a sudden wild tide,
indifferent, it seems, to the battle

of wind in the water;
for our blood, mixed
soon with their passion in sport,

in indifference, in anger,
will create new soils, new souls, new
ancestors; will flow like this tide fixed

to the star by which this ship floats
to new worlds, new waters, new
harbours, the pride of our ancestors mixed

with the wind and the water
the flesh and the flies, the whips and the fixed
fear of pain in this chained and welcoming port.

ALLEN CURNOW 1911–

LANDFALL IN UNKNOWN SEAS
The 300th Anniversary of the Discovery of New Zealand by Abel Tasman, 13 December 1642

I

Simply by sailing in a new direction
You could enlarge the world
                    You picked your captain,
Keen on discoveries, tough enough to make them,
Whatever vessels could be spared from other
More urgent service for a year's adventure;
Took stock of the more probable conjectures
About the Unknown to be traversed, all
Guesses at golden coasts and tales of monsters
To be digested into plain instructions
For likely and unlikely situations.

All this resolved and done, you launched the whole
On a fine morning, the best time of year,
Skies widening and the oceanic furies
Subdued by summer illumination; time
To go and to be gazed at going
On a fine morning, in the Name of God
Into the nameless waters of the world.

O you had estimated all the chances
Of business in those waters, the world's waters
Yet unexploited.
                    But more than the sea-empire's
Cannon, the dogs of bronze and iron barking
From Timor to the Straits, backed up the challenge.
Between you and the South an older enmity
Lodged in the searching mind, that would not tolerate

So huge a hegemony of ignorance.
There, where your Indies had already sprinkled
Their tribes like ocean rains, you aimed your voyage;
Like them invoked your God, gave seas to history
And islands to new hazardous tomorrows.

II

Suddenly exhilaration
Went off like a gun, the whole
Horizon, the long chase done,
Hove to. There was the seascape
Crammed with coast, surprising
As new lands will, the sailor
Moving on the face of the waters,
Watching the earth take shape
Round the unearthly summits, brighter
Than its emerging colour.

Yet this, no far fool's errand,
Was less than the heart desired,
In its old Indian dream
The glittering gulfs ascending
Past palaces and mountains
Making one architecture.
Here the uplifted structure,
Peak and pillar of cloud –
O splendour of desolation – reared
Tall from the pit of the swell,

With a shadow, a finger of wind, forbade
Hopes of a lucky landing.

Always to islanders danger
Is what comes over the sea;
Over the yellow sands and the clear
Shallows, the dull filament
Flickers, the blood of strangers:
Death discovered the Sailor
O in a flash, in a flat calm,
A clash of boats in the bay
And the day marred with murder.
The dead required no further
Warning to keep their distance;
The rest, noting the failure,
Pushed on with a reconnaissance
To the north; and sailed away.

III

Well, home is the Sailor, and that is a chapter
In a schoolbook, a relevant yesterday
We thought we knew all about, being much apter
   To profit, sure of our ground,
No murderers mooring in our Golden Bay.

But now there are no more islands to be found
And the eye scans risky horizons of its own
In unsettled weather, and murmurs of the drowned
   Haunt their familiar beaches –
Who navigates us towards what unknown

But not improbable provinces? Who reaches
A future down for us from the high shelf
Of spiritual daring? Not those speeches
    Pinning on the Past like a decoration
For merit that congratulates itself,

O not the self-important celebration
Or most painstaking history, can release
The current of a discoverer's elation
    And silence the voices saying,
'Here is the world's end where wonders cease.'

Only by a more faithful memory, laying
On him the half-light of a diffident glory,
The Sailor lives, and stands beside us, paying
    Out into our time's wave
The stain of blood that writes an island story.

OGDEN NASH 1902–71

COLUMBUS

Once upon a time there was an Italian,
And some people thought he was a rapscallion,
But he wasn't offended,
Because other people thought he was splendid,
And he said the world was round,
And everybody made an uncomplimentary sound,
But he went and tried to borrow some money from Ferdinand
But Ferdinand said America was a bird in the bush and he'd rather
    have a berdinand,
But Columbus' brain was fertile, it wasn't arid,
And he remembered that Ferdinand was married,
And he thought, there is no wife like a misunderstood one,
Because if her husband thinks something is a terrible idea she is bound
    to think it a good one,
So he perfumed his handkerchief with bay rum and citronella,
And he went to see Isabella,
And he looked wonderful but he had never felt sillier,
And she said, I can't place the face but the aroma is familiar,
And Columbus didn't say a word,
All he said was, I am Columbus, the fifteenth-century Admiral Byrd,
And, just as he thought, her disposition was very malleable,
And she said, Here are my jewels, and she wasn't penurious like
    Cornelia the mother of the Gracchi, she wasn't referring to her
    children, no, she was referring to her jewels, which were very very
    valuable,
So Columbus said, Somebody show me the sunset and somebody did
    and he set sail for it,
And he discovered America and they put him in jail for it,
And the fetters gave him welts,
And they named America after somebody else,
So the sad fate of Columbus ought to be pointed out to every child
    and every voter,
Because it has a very important moral, which is, Don't be a discoverer,
    be a promoter.

ELIZABETH BISHOP 1911–79

ARRIVAL AT SANTOS

Here is a coast; here is a harbour;
here, after a meagre diet of horizon, is some scenery:
impractically shaped and – who knows? – self-pitying mountains,
sad and harsh beneath their frivolous greenery,

with a little church on top of one. And warehouses,
some of them painted a feeble pink, or blue,
and some tall, uncertain palms. Oh, tourist,
is this how this country is going to answer you

and your immodest demands for a different world,
and a better life, and complete comprehension
of both at last, and immediately,
after eighteen days of suspension?

Finish your breakfast. The tender is coming,
a strange and ancient craft, flying a strange and brilliant rag.
So that's the flag. I never saw it before.
I somehow never thought of there *being* a flag,

but of course there was, all along. And coins, I presume,
and paper money; they remain to be seen.
And gingerly now we climb down the ladder backward,
myself and a fellow passenger named Miss Breen,

descending into the midst of twenty-six freighters
waiting to be loaded with green coffee beans.
Please, boy, do be more careful with that boat hook!
Watch out! Oh! It has caught Miss Breen's

skirt! There! Miss Breen is about seventy,
a retired police lieutenant, six feet tall,
with beautiful bright blue eyes and a kind expression.
Her home, when she is at home, is in Glens Fall

s, New York. There. We are settled.
The customs officials will speak English, we hope,
and leave us our bourbon and cigarettes.
Ports are necessities, like postage stamps, or soap,

but they seldom seem to care what impression they make,
or, like this, only attempt, since it does not matter,
the unassertive colours of soap, or postage stamps –
wasting away like the former, slipping the way the latter

do when we mail the letters we wrote on the boat,
either because the glue here is very inferior
or because of the heat. We leave Santos at once;
we are driving to the interior.

ALAN BROWNJOHN 1931–

FOR A JOURNEY

House Field, Top Field, Oak Field, Third Field:
Though maps conclude their duties, the names trek on
Unseen across every county. Farmers call hillocks
And ponds and streams and lanes and rocks
By the first words to hand; a heavy, whittled-down
Simplicity meets the need, enough to help say
Where has yielded best, or the way they walked from home.

You can travel safely over land so named –
Where there is nowhere that could not somewhere
Be found in a memory which knows, and loves.
So watch then, all the more carefully, for
The point where the pattern ends: where mountains, even,
And swamps and forests and gaping bays acquire
The air of not needing ever to be spoken of.

Who knows what could become of you where
No one has understood the place with names?

'And as the twilight nets the plunging sun
My heart's keel slides to rest among the meadows.'

from 'Home from Abroad'

LAURIE LEE 1914–97

HOME FROM ABROAD

Far-fetched with tales of other worlds and ways,
My skin well-oiled with wines of the Levant,
I set my face into a filial smile
To greet the pale, domestic kiss of Kent.

But shall I never learn? That gawky girl,
Recalled so primly in my foreign thoughts,
Becomes again the green-haired queen of love
Whose wanton form dilates as it delights.

Her rolling tidal landscape floods the eye
And drowns Chianti in a dusky stream;
The flower-flecked grasses swim with simple horses,
The hedges choke with roses fat as cream.

So do I breathe the hayblown airs of home,
And watch the sea-green elms drip birds and shadows,
And as the twilight nets the plunging sun
My heart's keel slides to rest among the meadows.

DEREK MAHON 1941–

from AFTERLIVES
For James Simmons

2

I am going home by sea
For the first time in years.
Somebody thumbs a guitar
On the dark deck, while a gull
Dreams at the masthead,
The moon-splashed waves exult.

At dawn the ship trembles, turns
In a wide arc to back
Shuddering up the grey lough
Past lightship and buoy,
Slipway and dry dock
Where a naked bulb burns;

And I step ashore in a fine rain
To a city so changed
By five years of war
I scarcely recognize
The places I grew up in,
The faces that try to explain.

But the hills are still the same
Grey-blue above Belfast.
Perhaps if I'd stayed behind
And lived it bomb by bomb
I might have grown up at last
And learnt what is meant by home.

KEITH DOUGLAS 1920–44

ON A RETURN FROM EGYPT

To stand here in the wings of Europe
disheartened, I have come away
from the sick land where in the sun lay
the gentle sloe-eyed murderers
of themselves, exquisites under a curse;
here to exercise my depleted fury.

For the heart is a coal, growing colder
when jewelled cerulean seas change
into grey rocks, grey water-fringe,
sea and sky altering like a cloth
till colour and sheen are gone both:
cold is an opiate of the soldier.

And all my endeavours are unlucky explorers
come back, abandoning the expedition;
the specimens, the lilies of ambition
still spring in their climate, still unpicked:
but time, time is all I lacked
to find them, as the great collectors before me.

The next month, then, is a window
and with a crash I'll split the glass.
Behind it stands one I must kiss,
person of love or death
a person or a wraith,
I fear what I shall find.

                              Egypt–England, 1943–44.

LOUIS MACNEICE 1907–63

from AUTUMN JOURNAL

VI

And I remember Spain
    At Easter ripe as an egg for revolt and ruin
Though for a tripper the rain
    Was worse than the surly or the worried or the haunted faces
With writings on the walls –
    Hammer and sickle, Boicot, Viva, Muerra;
With café-au-lait brimming the waterfalls,
    With sherry, shellfish, omelettes.
With fretted stone the Moor
    Had chiselled for effects of sun and shadow;
With shadows of the poor,
    The begging cripples and the children begging.
The churches full of saints
    Tortured on racks of marble –
The old complaints
    Covered with gilt and dimly lit with candles.
With powerful or banal
    Monuments of riches or repression
And the Escorial
    Cold for ever within like the heart of Philip.
With ranks of dominoes
    Deployed on café tables the whole of Sunday;
With cabarets that call the tourist, shows
    Of thighs and eyes and nipples.
With slovenly soldiers, nuns,
    And peeling posters from the last elections
Promising bread or guns
    Or an amnesty or another
Order or else the old
    Glory veneered and varnished
As if veneer could hold
    The rotten guts and crumbled bones together.
And a vulture hung in air

115

Below the cliffs of Ronda and below him
His hook-winged shadow wavered like despair
   Across the chequered vineyards.
And the boot-blacks in Madrid
   Kept us half an hour with polish and pincers
And all we did
   In that city was drink and think and loiter.
And in the Prado half-
   wit princes looked from the canvas they had paid for
(Goya had the laugh –
   But can what is corrupt be cured by laughter?)
And the day at Aranjuez
   When the sun came out for once on the yellow river
With Valdepeñas burdening the breath
   We slept a royal sleep in the royal gardens;
And at Toledo walked
   Around the ramparts where they throw the garbage
And glibly talked
   Of how the Spaniards lack all sense of business.
And Avila was cold
   And Segovia was picturesque and smelly
And a goat on the road seemed old
   As the rocks or the Roman arches.
And Easter was wet and full
   In Seville and in the ring on Easter Sunday
A clumsy bull and then a clumsy bull
   Nodding his banderillas died of boredom.
And the standard of living was low
   But that, we thought to ourselves, was not our business;
All that the tripper wants is the *status quo*
   Cut and dried for trippers.
And we thought the papers a lark
   With their party politics and blank invective;

And we thought the dark
    Women who dyed their hair should have it dyed more often.
And we sat in trains all night
    With the windows shut among civil guards and peasants
And tried to play piquet by a tiny light
    And tried to sleep bolt upright;
And cursed the Spanish rain
    And cursed their cigarettes which came to pieces
And caught heavy colds in Cordova and in vain
    Waited for the right light for taking photos.
And we met a Cambridge don who said with an air
    'There's going to be trouble shortly in this country,'
And ordered anis, pudgy and debonair,
    Glad to show off his mastery of the language.
But only an inch behind
    This map of olive and ilex, this painted hoarding,
Careless of visitors the people's mind
    Was tunnelling like a mole to day and danger.
And the day before we left
    We saw the mob in flower at Algeciras
Outside a toothless door, a church bereft
    Of its images and its aura.
And at La Linea while
    The night put miles between us and Gibraltar
We heard the blood-lust of a drunkard pile
    His heaven high with curses;
And next day took the boat
    For home, forgetting Spain, not realizing
That Spain would soon denote
    Our grief, our aspirations;
Not knowing that our blunt
    Ideals would find their whetstone, that our spirit
Would find its frontier on the Spanish front,
    Its body in a rag-tag army.

RUTHVEN TODD 1914–

IN SEPTEMBER

Coming, in September, through the thin streets,
I thought back to another year I knew,
Autumn, lifting potatoes and stacking peats
On Mull, while the Atlantic's murky blue
Swung sluggishly in past Jura, and the hills
Were brown lions, crouched to meet the autumn gales.

In the hard rain and the rip of thunder,
I remembered the haze coming in from the sea
And the clatter of Gaelic voices by the breakwater
Or in the fields as the reapers took their tea;
I remembered the cast foal lying where it died,
Which we buried, one evening, above high-tide;

And the three rams that smashed the fank-gate,
Running loose for five days on the moor
Before we could catch them – far too late
To prevent an early lambing the next year.
But these seemed out of place beside the chip-shop
And the cockney voices grumbling in the pub.

In September, I saw the drab newsposters
Telling of wars, in Spain and in the East,
And wished I'd stayed on Mull, their gestures
Frightened me and made me feel the unwanted guest.
The burden on the house who having taken salt
Could never be ejected, however grave his fault.

In September, we lit the fire and talked together,
Discussing the trivialities of a spent day
And what we would eat. I forgot the weather
And the dull streets and the sun on Islay,
And all my fear. I lost my carefully-kept count
Of the ticks to death, and, in September, was content.

BERNARD GUTTERIDGE 1916–

HOME REVISITED

Now that I go there as a visitor,
To the end of the thin lane,
And pass the rockery with a stranger
Walk, I can recall his death again.

Birth and death identically change
While the house remains the same;
Grow from a boyhood's sword-sharp lunge
Of fear and love to an imagist's game.

Birth as the red-ribboning of a cot,
An unknown nurse in a rage;
As the seven swallows that sit
Dropping their pellets on the saxifrage

That wags its racket seed pods in the wind
Rotting brownly from the centre;
The doctor's shadow on the blind,
Spring summer autumn or winter.

Death as my walking past this empty shell:
The fixed memory of life
Ceasing like echoes in a well
Beyond the last ripple of short grief.

Death as a circle of nettles where the hut
Turned the patient to the wind.
That wind has taken seeds and set
Dock leaves' tusk roots into the heavy ground,

Or as the untidy nests the starlings build
To for ever leave and enter;
The doctor's shadow on the blind,
Spring summer autumn or winter.

DANNIE ABSE 1923–

from CAR JOURNEYS

1. Down the M4

Me! dutiful son going back to South Wales, this time afraid
to hear my mother's news. Too often, now, her friends are disrobed,
and my aunts and uncles, too, go into the hole, one by one.
The beautiful face of my mother is in its ninth decade.

Each visit she tells me the monotonous story of clocks.
'Oh dear,' I say, or 'how funny,' till I feel my hair turning grey
for I've heard that perishable one two hundred times before –
like the rugby 'amateurs' with golden sovereigns in their socks.

Then the Tawe ran fluent and trout-coloured over stones stonier,
more genuine; then Annabella, my mother's mother, spoke Welsh
with such an accent the village said, 'Tell the truth, fach,
you're no Jewess. *They're* from the Bible. *You're* from Patagonia!'

I'm driving down the M4 again under bridges that leap
over me then shrink in my side mirror. Ystalyfera is farther
than smoke and God further than all distance known. I whistle
no hymn but an Old Yiddish tune my mother knows. It won't keep.

PETER HEWETT 1914–92

PLACE OF BIRTH

From Winchester the road was dazed with heat
after the droughty downs the lanes were night
and drowned in leaves across their cakey ruts:
down through the hedge's tunnel and the dust
lay my small village huddling in its trees.

Unmoved since twenty-two its settled houses
however tiny to my later eyes
the fields the trees the bushes seemed the same
as when I left them in that dreaded April:
and though the men were dead or gone to Norwich
the women bedridden, the children married,
yet with the known road under my older feet
familiar cowsheds and remembered lanes
swooped back to me those misty years
when Hampshire was my home and London lovely.

The cottage squatted in its tangled garden
condemned for years to rot and sink:
the thatch was mossy and the well was rust
the hollow hogweed grew beside the barn
where the late sun was setting through the cracks
and redhead docks stood in the living-room
against the curling paper on the wall
towards the ceiling's plaster and its stains:
I picked a plum from the forgotten tree
and wordless smells hung in the evening air
telling me I was eight, the school was finished,
through the long grass the twisty path, and home
was the small chimney down the valley's blue.

Here I was reared: these fields were mine for running
these beechy lanes my setting and my soil
a solemn boy with knees and canvas satchels . . .

the milkcan handle cold in Christmas snow
the plovers howling ghosts against the wind:
the larches in the copse were paintbox colours
and the red admirals hovered on the ivy:
the autumn brought its gleaning in the stubble
and apples drooping by the window pane.

This was my world, this unconsidered corner
and a long journey was a league away
through fields to Baybridge or to Fisher's Pond:
London was at the Pole, a kindly giant
with angel porters and tremendous trams:
and here I watched and walked, while vast unknown
history swept by, and blood in Ireland
war on the Soviets, Sacco in his gaol,
crises, indemnities, putsches and revolts . . .
and I unseeing in my woods, happy in knowing
peace on the skyline and the future firm.

We weep for what is gone: my dying dog
is the pathetic puppy in the market cage;
never again that long oblivious calm
and yet our tears for loss, the dying years
the sun and colour of the spacious past:
and tonight's misty trees and mackerel sky
remembered in the draughty days to come
tearing at hearts shaken by midnight guns.

*'Whose dream is this, I would like to know:
is this a manufactured
hallucination,'*

       from 'At the Tourist Center in Boston'

W. B. YEATS 1865–1939

SAILING TO BYZANTIUM

I

That is no country for old men. The young
In one another's arms, birds in the trees
– Those dying generations – at their song,
The salmon-falls, the mackerel-crowded seas,
Fish, flesh, or fowl, commend all summer long
Whatever is begotten, born, and dies.
Caught in that sensual music all neglect
Monuments of unaging intellect.

II

An aged man is but a paltry thing,
A tattered coat upon a stick, unless
Soul clap its hands and sing, and louder sing
For every tatter in its mortal dress,
Nor is there singing school but studying
Monuments of its own magnificence;
And therefore I have sailed the seas and come
To the holy city of Byzantium.

III

O sages standing in God's holy fire
As in the gold mosaic of a wall,
Come from the holy fire, perne in a gyre,
And be the singing-masters of my soul.
Consume my heart away; sick with desire
And fastened to a dying animal
It knows not what it is; and gather me
Into the artifice of eternity.

IV

Once out of nature I shall never take
My bodily form from any natural thing,
But such a form as Grecian goldsmiths make
Of hammered gold and gold enamelling
To keep a drowsy Emperor awake;
Or set upon a golden bough to sing
To lords and ladies of Byzantium
Of what is past, or passing, or to come.

PERCY BYSSHE SHELLEY 1792–1822

OZYMANDIAS

I met a traveller from an antique land
Who said: Two vast and trunkless legs of stone
Stand in the desert . . . Near them, on the sand,
Half sunk, a shattered visage lies, whose frown,
And wrinkled lip, and sneer of cold command,
Tell that its sculptor well those passions read
Which yet survive, stamped on these lifeless things,
The hand that mocked them, and the heart that fed:
And on the pedestal these words appear:
'My name is Ozymandias, king of kings:
Look on my works, ye Mighty, and despair!'
Nothing beside remains. Round the decay
Of that colossal wreck, boundless and bare
The lone and level sands stretch far away.

JOHN KEATS 1795–1821

ON FIRST LOOKING INTO CHAPMAN'S HOMER

Much have I travelled in the realms of gold,
    And many goodly states and kingdoms seen;
    Round many western islands have I been
Which bards in fealty to Apollo hold.
Oft of one wide expanse had I been told
    That deep-browed Homer ruled as his demesne;
    Yet did I never breathe its pure serene
Till I heard Chapman speak out loud and bold:
Then felt I like some watcher of the skies
    When a new planet swims into his ken;
Or like stout Cortez when with eagle eyes
    He stared at the Pacific – and all his men
Looked at each other with a wild surmise –
    Silent, upon a peak in Darien.

W. B. YEATS 1865–1939

THE LAKE ISLE OF INNISFREE

I will arise and go now, and go to Innisfree,
And a small cabin build there, of clay and wattles made:
Nine bean-rows will I have there, a hive for the honey-bee,
And live alone in the bee-loud glade.

And I shall have some peace there, for peace comes dropping slow,
Dropping from the veils of the morning to where the cricket sings;
There midnight's all a glimmer, and noon a purple glow,
And evening full of the linnet's wings.

I will arise and go now, for always night and day
I hear lake water lapping with low sounds by the shore;
While I stand on the roadway, or on the pavements grey,
I hear it in the deep heart's core.

SAMUEL TAYLOR COLERIDGE 1772–1834

KUBLA KHAN

In Xanadu did Kubla Khan
A stately pleasure-dome decree:
Where Alph, the sacred river, ran
Through caverns measureless to man
  Down to a sunless sea.
So twice five miles of fertile ground
With walls and towers were girdled round:
And there were gardens bright with sinuous rills,
Where blossomed many an incense-bearing tree;
And here were forests ancient as the hills,
Enfolding sunny spots of greenery.

But oh! that deep romantic chasm which slanted
Down the green hill athwart a cedarn cover!
A savage place! as holy and enchanted
As e'er beneath a waning moon was haunted
By woman wailing for her demon-lover!
And from this chasm, with ceaseless turmoil seething,
As if this earth in fast thick pants were breathing,
A mighty fountain momently was forced:
Amid whose swift half-intermitted burst
Huge fragments vaulted like rebounding hail,
Or chaffy grain beneath the thresher's flail:
And 'mid these dancing rocks at once and ever
It flung up momently the sacred river.
Five miles meandering with a mazy motion
Through wood and dale the sacred river ran,
Then reached the caverns measureless to man,
And sank in tumult to a lifeless ocean:
And 'mid this tumult Kubla heard from far
Ancestral voices prophesying war!
    The shadow of the dome of pleasure
    Floated midway on the waves;
    Where was heard the mingled measure

From the fountain and the caves.
It was a miracle of rare device,
A sunny pleasure-dome with caves of ice!

A damsel with a dulcimer
In a vision once I saw:
It was an Abyssinian maid,
And on her dulcimer she played,
Singing of Mount Abora.
Could I revive within me
Her symphony and song,
To such a deep delight 'twould win me,
That with music loud and long,
I would build that dome in air,
That sunny dome! those caves of ice!
And all who heard should see them there,
And all should cry, Beware! Beware!
His flashing eyes, his floating hair!
Weave a circle round him thrice,
And close your eyes with holy dread,
For he on honey-dew hath fed,
And drunk the milk of Paradise.

EDWARD LEAR 1812–88

THE OWL AND THE PUSSY-CAT

I

The Owl and the Pussy-cat went to sea
  In a beautiful pea-green boat,
They took some honey, and plenty of money,
  Wrapped up in a five-pound note.
The Owl looked up to the stars above,
  And sang to a small guitar,
'O lovely Pussy! O Pussy, my love,
  What a beautiful Pussy you are,
    You are,
    You are!
  What a beautiful Pussy you are!'

II

Pussy said to the Owl, 'You elegant fowl!
  How charmingly sweet you sing!
O let us be married! too long we have tarried:
  But what shall we do for a ring?'
They sailed away, for a year and a day,
  To the land where the Bong-tree grows
And there in a wood a Piggy-wig stood
  With a ring at the end of his nose,
    His nose,
    His nose,
  With a ring at the end of his nose.

III

'Dear Pig, are willing to sell for one shilling
  Your ring?' Said the Piggy, 'I will.'
So they took it away, and were married next day
  By the Turkey who lives on the hill.
They dined on mince, and slices of quince,

Which they ate with a runcible spoon;
And hand in hand, on the edge of the sand,
They danced by the light of the moon,
    The moon,
    The moon,
They danced by the light of the moon.

THOM GUNN 1929–

A MAP OF THE CITY

I stand upon a hill and see
A luminous country under me,
Through which at two the drunk must weave;
The transient's pause, the sailor's leave.

I notice, looking down the hill,
Arms braced upon a window sill;
And on the web of fire escapes
Move the potential, the grey shapes.

I hold the city here, complete:
And every shape defined by light
Is mine, or corresponds to mine,
Some flickering or some steady shine.

This map is ground of my delight.
Between the limits, night by night,
I watch a malady's advance,
I recognize my love of chance.

By the recurrent lights I see
Endless potentiality,
The crowded, broken, and unfinished!
I would not have the risk diminished.

MARGARET ATWOOD 1939–

AT THE TOURIST CENTER IN BOSTON

There is my country under glass,
a white relief-
map with red dots for the cities,
reduced to the size of a wall

and beside it 10 blownup snapshots
one for each province,
in purple-browns and odd reds,
the green of the trees dulled;
all blues however
of an assertive purity.

Mountains and lakes and more lakes
(though Quebec is a restaurant and Ontario the empty
interior of the parliament buildings),
with nobody climbing the trails and hauling out
the fish and splashing in the water

but arrangements of grinning tourists –
look here, Saskatchewan
is a flat lake, some convenient rocks
where two children pose with a father
and the mother is cooking something
in immaculate slacks by a smokeless fire,
her teeth white as detergent.

Whose dream is this, I would like to know:
is this a manufactured
hallucination, a cynical fiction, a lure
for export only?

I seem to remember people,
at least in the cities, also slush,
machines and assorted garbage. Perhaps
    that was my private mirage

which will just evaporate
when I go back. Or the citizens will be gone,
run off to the peculiarly-
green forests
to wait among the brownish mountains
for the platoons of tourists
and plan their odd red massacres.

Unsuspecting
window lady, I ask you:

Do you see nothing
watching you from under the water?

Was the sky ever that blue?

Who really lives there?

SHEENAGH PUGH 1950–

'DO YOU THINK WE'LL EVER GET TO SEE EARTH, SIR?'

I hear they're hoping to run trips
one day, for the young and fit, of course.
I don't see much use in it myself;
there'll be any number of places
you can't land, because they're still toxic,
and even in the relatively safe bits
you won't see what it was; what it could be.
I can't fancy a tour through the ruins
of my home with a party of twenty-five
and a guide to tell me what to see.
But if you should see some beautiful thing,
some leaf, say, damascened with frost,
some iridescence on a pigeon's neck,
some stone, some curve, some clear water;
look at it as if you were made of eyes,
as if you were nothing but an eye, lidless
and tender, to be probed and scorched
by extreme light. Look at it with your skin,
with the small hairs on the back of your neck.
If it is well-shaped, look at it with your hands;
if it has fragrance, breathe it into yourself;
if it tastes sweet, put your tongue to it.
Look at it as a happening, a moment;
let nothing of it go unrecorded,
map it as if it were already passing.
Look at it with the inside of your head,
look at it for later, look at it for ever,
and look at it once for me.

VERNON SCANNELL 1922–

NO SENSE OF DIRECTION

I have always admired
Those who are sure
Which turning to take,
Who need no guide
Even in war
When thunders shake
The torn terrain,
When battalions of shrill
Stars all desert
And the derelict moon
Goes over the hill:
Eyes chained by the night
They find their way back
As if it were daylight.
Then, on peaceful walks
Over strange wooded ground,
They will find the right track,
Know which of the forks
Will lead to the inn
I would never have found;
For I lack their gift,
Possess almost no
Sense of direction.
And yet I owe
A debt to this lack,
A debt so vast
No reparation
Can ever be made,
For it led me away
From the road I sought

Which would carry me to –
I mistakenly thought –
My true destination:
It made me stray
To this lucky path
That ran like a fuse
And brought me to you
And love's bright, soundless
Detonation.

'*And I rose*
In rainy autumn
And walked abroad in a shower of all my days.'

from 'Poem in October'

WILLIAM SHAKESPEARE 1564–1616

SONNET LX

Like as the waves make towards the pebbled shore,
　So do our minutes hasten to their end;
Each changing place with that which goes before,
　In sequent toil all forwards do contend.
Nativity, once in the main of light,
　Crawls to maturity, wherewith being crowned,
Crooked eclipses 'gainst his glory fight,
　And Time that gave doth now his gift confound.
Time doth transfix the flourish set on youth
　And delves the parallels in beauty's brow,
Feeds on the rarities of nature's truth,
　And nothing stands but for his scythe to mow.
　　And yet to times in hope my verse shall stand,
　　Praising thy worth, despite his cruel hand.

ROBERT BROWNING 1812–89

TWO IN THE CAMPAGNA

I

I wonder do you feel today
    As I have felt since, hand in hand,
We sat down on the grass, to stray
    In spirit better through the land,
This morn of Rome and May?

II

For me, I touched a thought, I know,
    Has tantalized me many times,
(Like turns of thread the spiders throw
    Mocking across our path) for rhymes
To catch at and let go.

III

Help me to hold it! First it left
    The yellowing fennel, run to seed
There, branching from the brickwork's cleft,
    Some old tomb's ruin: yonder weed
Took up the floating weft,

IV

Where one small orange cup amassed
    Five beetles – blind and green they grope
Among the honey-meal: and last,
    Everywhere on the grassy slope
I traced it. Hold it fast!

V

The champaign with its endless fleece
    Of feathery grasses everywhere!

Silence and passion, joy and peace,
    An everlasting wash of air –
Rome's ghost since her decease.

VI

Such life here, through such lengths of hours,
    Such miracles performed in play,
Such primal naked forms of flowers,
    Such letting nature have her way
While heaven looks from its towers!

VII

How say you? Let us, O my dove,
    Let us be unashamed of soul,
As earth lies bare to heaven above!
    How is it under our control
To love or not to love?

VIII

I would that you were all to me,
    You that are just so much, no more.
Nor yours nor mine, nor slave nor free!
    Where does the fault lie? What the core
O' the wound, since wound must be?

IX

I would I could adopt your will,
    See with your eyes, and set my heart
Beating by yours, and drink my fill
    At your soul's springs – your part my part
In life, for good and ill.

X

No. I yearn upward, touch you close,
    Then stand away. I kiss your cheek,
Catch your soul's warmth – I pluck the rose
    And love it more than tongue can speak –
Then the good minute goes.

XI

Already how am I so far
    Out of that minute? Must I go
Still like the thistle-ball, no bar,
    Onward, whenever light winds blow,
Fixed by no friendly star?

XII

Just when I seemed about to learn!
    Where is the thread now? Off again!
The old trick! Only I discern –
    Infinite passion, and the pain
Of finite hearts that yearn.

ANDREW MOTION 1952–

from BLOODLINES

I. Bro

We walked the way we had seen
our elders and betters walk
on their and their families' land:
with a head-back swaggering stride,
our hands stuffed deep in our pockets,

and pushed through a scraggy hedge
in the pewter afternoon light
to come to a spongy meadow
dotted with carious Cotswold boulders.
They'd told us to disappear

and discover the source of the Thames,
making us think we might find
a god stretched in a thicket
whose mouth was a massive O
spewing the river out into the grass.

But someone had stolen the god,
or maybe he never existed.
Instead we came to a patch
of stubbly reed where water
convulsed like a catch of mackerel,

and this, we supposed, was it.
We knew there was nothing to do
but quickly to match the pretence
of our head-back brazen approach
with a faked-up sense of arrival,

and stood there in silence for a while,
watching the water swallow its tails.
Whatever came into your mind
was something you never said then,
and soon it was too late to ask

since a matter of days after that
I was parcelled away to school,
and took, as if it belonged to me,
the thought of the river collecting
the strength of a million ditches

hungrily under the ground,
emerging to shoulder through Lechlade,
and Oxford, and London, oily with prints
of tug-boats, and hurrying half-blind faces
peering from bridges, and giggling couples

throwing in twigs and watching them
wriggle from sight in curdling eddies,
and marvellous nineteenth-century walls
built right at the water's edge, so the eyes
of their gargoyles stare at themselves for ever.

JAMES KIRKUP 1923–

WAITING FOR THE TRAIN TO START

The mysterious movement of a dream
came back to my awakened sense
that evening, in the apparent gliding
of the stationary train, in which alone
I waited, watching the slow start,
the wheel withdrawal and increasing
miracle of effort of the long, sustained
acceleration as the sleeping cars,
the dim, flickering procession
of the train that had been still
beside me, eased itself without a sign
away, in yet another stern departure.

As I watched it, from my half-dark corner,
with the other train's departure I
too seemed to move, and swiftly slide,
but in departure more than ordinary,
sadder, more intense than any past farewell.
For I, too, but in the opposite direction
was departing, with the same ingrowing
pain of speed, yet with a dream's haunted sense
of motion without feeling, speed
without the sound and energy of wings labouring
in the materials of space and time, an ever backwards hauled
propulsion, memory of birth and future things.

Soon, in this earth-borne flight,
this effortless commotion, powerless,
but faint with force that seemed to spell
a vast and irresistible vanishment,

my eyes half closed, in heavenly suspense
my weightless body came adrift,
and on a wind's great soundless sea
of sense and spirit it was smoothly launched . . .
Until time and the final carriage crashed
reality awake again. As if from a real dream
from real heights out of myself I leaped, and fell
back into stationary blackness, and my heart's loud hell.

RUDYARD KIPLING 1865–1936

THE WAY THROUGH THE WOODS

They shut the road through the woods
Seventy years ago.
Weather and rain have undone it again,
And now you would never know
There was once a road through the woods
Before they planted the trees.
It is underneath the coppice and heath
And the thin anemones.
Only the keeper sees
That, where the ring-dove broods,
And the badgers roll at ease,
There was once a road through the woods.

Yet, if you enter the woods
Of a summer evening late,
When the night-air cools on the trout-ringed pools
Where the otter whistles his mate,
(They fear not men in the woods,
Because they see so few.)
You will hear the beat of a horse's feet,
And the swish of a skirt in the dew,
Steadily cantering through
The misty solitudes,
As though they perfectly knew
The old lost road through the woods. . . .
But there is no road through the woods.

DYLAN THOMAS 1914–53

POEM IN OCTOBER

It was my thirtieth year to heaven
Woke to my hearing from harbour and neighbour wood
  And the mussel pooled and the heron
      Priested shore
     The morning beckon
With water praying and call of seagull and rook
And the knock of sailing boats on the net webbed wall
    Myself to set foot
     That second
  In the still sleeping town and set forth.

My birthday began with the water-
Birds and the birds of the winged trees flying my name
  Above the farms and the white horses
     And I rose
    In rainy autumn
And walked abroad in a shower of all my days.
High tide and the heron dived when I took the road
    Over the border
     And the gates
  Of the town closed as the town awoke.

A springful of larks in a rolling
Cloud and the roadside bushes brimming with whistling
  Blackbirds and the sun of October
     Summery
    On the hill's shoulder,
Here were fond climates and sweet singers suddenly
Come in the morning where I wandered and listened
    To the rain wringing
     Wind blow cold
  In the wood faraway under me.

Pale rain over the dwindling harbour
And over the sea wet church the size of a snail
  With its horns through mist and the castle
      Brown as owls
    But all the gardens
Of spring and summer were blooming in the tall tales
Beyond the border and under the lark full cloud.
    There could I marvel
      My birthday
Away but the weather turned around.

It turned away from the blithe country
And down the other air and the blue altered sky
  Streamed again a wonder of summer
      With apples
    Pears and red currants
And I saw in the turning so clearly a child's
Forgotten mornings when he walked with his mother
    Through the parables
      Of sun light
And the legends of the green chapels.

And the twice told fields of infancy
That his tears burned my cheeks and his heart moved in mine.
  These were the woods the river and sea
      Where a boy
    In the listening
Summertime of the dead whispered the truth of his joy
To the trees and the stones and the fish in the tide.
    And the mystery
      Sang alive
Still in the water and singingbirds.

And there could I marvel my birthday
Away but the weather turned around. And the true
  Joy of the long dead child sang burning
        In the sun.
       It was my thirtieth
Year to heaven stood there then in the summer noon
Though the town below lay leaved with October blood.
      O may my heart's truth
        Still be sung
   On this high hill in a year's turning.

'*Then am I ready, like a palmer fit,*
To tread those blest paths which before I writ.'

from 'The Passionate Man's Pilgrimage'

GEOFFREY CHAUCER *c.* 1343–1400

from THE CANTERBURY TALES

THE GENERAL PROLOGUE

Whan that April with his showres soote
The droughte of March hath perced to the roote,
And bathed every veine in swich licour,
Of which vertu engendred is the flowr;
Whan Zephyrus eek with his sweete breeth
Inspired hath in every holt and heeth
The tendre croppes, and the yonge sonne
Hath in the Ram his halve cours yronne,
And smale fowles maken melodye
That sleepen al the night with open yë –
So priketh hem Nature in hir corages –
Thanne longen folk to goon on pilgrimages,
And palmeres for to seeken straunge strondes
To ferne halwes, couthe in sondry londes;
And specially from every shires ende
Of Engelond to Canterbury they wende,
The holy blisful martyr for to seeke
That hem hath holpen whan that they were seke.
  Bifel that in that seson on a day,
In Southwerk at the Tabard as I lay,
Redy to wenden on my pilgrimage
To Canterbury with ful devout corage,
At night was come into that hostelrye
Wel nine and twenty in a compaignye
Of sondry folk, by aventure yfalle
In felaweshipe, and pilgrimes were they alle
That toward Canterbury wolden ride.
The chambres and the stables weren wide,

And wel we weren esed at the beste.
And shortly, whan the sonne was to reste,
So hadde I spoken with hem everichoon
That I was of hir felaweshipe anoon,
    And made forward erly for to rise,
    To take oure way ther as I you devise.

T. S. ELIOT 1888–1965

JOURNEY OF THE MAGI

'A cold coming we had of it,
Just the worst time of the year
For a journey, and such a long journey:
The ways deep and the weather sharp,
The very dead of winter.'
And the camels galled, sore-footed, refractory,
Lying down in the melting snow.
There were times we regretted
The summer palaces on slopes, the terraces,
And the silken girls bringing sherbet.
Then the camel men cursing and grumbling
And running away, and wanting their liquor and women,
And the night-fires going out, and the lack of shelters,
And the cities hostile and the towns unfriendly
And the villages dirty and charging high prices:
A hard time we had of it.
At the end we preferred to travel all night,
Sleeping in snatches,
With the voices singing in our ears, saying
That this was all folly.

Then at dawn we came down to a temperate valley,
Wet, below the snow line, smelling of vegetation;
With a running stream and a water-mill beating the darkness,
And three trees on the low sky,
And an old white horse galloped away in the meadow.
Then we came to a tavern with vine-leaves over the lintel,
Six hands at an open door dicing for pieces of silver,
And feet kicking the empty wine-skins.
But there was no information, and so we continued
And arrived at evening, not a moment too soon
Finding the place; it was (you may say) satisfactory.

All this was a long time ago, I remember,
And I would do it again, but set down
This set down
This: were we led all that way for
Birth or Death? There was a Birth, certainly,
We had evidence and no doubt. I had seen birth and death,
But had thought they were different; this Birth was
Hard and bitter agony for us, like Death, our death.
We returned to our places, these Kingdoms,
But no longer at ease here, in the old dispensation,
With an alien people clutching their gods.
I should be glad of another death.

JOHN DONNE 1572–1631

GOOD FRIDAY, 1613. RIDING WESTWARD

Let man's soul be a sphere, and then, in this,
The'intelligence that moves, devotion is,
And as the other spheres, by being grown
Subject to foreign motions, lose their own,
And being by others hurried every day,
Scarce in a year their natural form obey;
Pleasure or business, so, our souls admit
For their first mover, and are whirled by it.
Hence is 't, that I am carried towards the West
This day, when my soul's form bends towards the East.
There I should see a Sun, by rising, set,
And by that setting endless day beget;
But that Christ on this cross did rise and fall,
Sin had eternally benighted all.
Yet dare I'almost be glad I do not see
That spectacle, of too much weight for me.
Who sees God's face, that is self-life, must die;
What a death were it then to see God die?
It made his own lieutenant, Nature, shrink;
It made his footstool crack, and the sun wink.
Could I behold those hands which span the poles,
And tune all spheres at once, pierced with those holes?
Could I behold that endless height which is
Zenith to us, and to'our antipodes,
Humbled below us? Or that blood which is
The seat of all our souls, if not of His,
Make dirt of dust, or that flesh which was worn
By God, for his apparel, ragg'd and torn?
If on these things I durst not look, durst I
Upon his miserable mother cast mine eye,
Who was God's partner here, and furnished thus
Half of that sacrifice which ransomed us?
Though these things, as I ride, be from mine eye,
They're present yet unto my memory,

For that looks towards them; and thou look'st towards me,
O Saviour, as thou hang'st upon the tree.
I turn my back to thee but to receive
Corrections, till thy mercies bid thee leave.
O think me worth thine anger; punish me;
Burn off my rusts and my deformity;
Restore thine image so much, by thy grace,
That thou may'st know me, and I'll turn my face.

SIR WALTER RALEGH 1552–1618

THE PASSIONATE MAN'S PILGRIMAGE
posed to be written by One at the Point of Death

Give me my scallop-shell of quiet,
My staff of faith to walk upon,
My scrip of joy, immortal diet,
My bottle of salvation,
My gown of glory, hope's true gage,
And thus I'll take my pilgrimage.

Blood must be my body's balmer,
No other balm will there be given,
Whilst my soul like a white palmer
Travels to the land of heaven,
Over the silver mountains,
Where spring the nectar fountains;
And there I'll kiss
The bowl of bliss,
And drink my eternal fill
On every milken hill.
My soul will be a-dry before,
But after it will ne'er thirst more.

And by the happy blissful way
More peaceful pilgrims I shall see,
That have shook off their gowns of clay
And go apparelled fresh like me.
I'll bring them first
To slake their thirst,
And then to taste those nectar suckets,
At the clear wells
Where sweetness dwells,
Drawn up by saints in crystal buckets.

And when our bottles and all we
Are filled with immortality,
Then the holy paths we'll travel,
Strewed with rubies thick as gravel,
Ceilings of diamonds, sapphire floors,
High walls of coral and pearl bowers.

From thence to heaven's bribeless hall
Where no corrupted voices brawl,
No conscience molten into gold,
Nor forged accusers bought and sold,
No cause deferred, nor vain-spent journey,
For there Christ is the King's Attorney,
Who pleads for all without degrees,
And he hath angels, but no fees.

When the grand twelve million jury
Of our sins with sinful fury
'Gainst our souls black verdicts give,
Christ pleads his death, and then we live.
Be thou my speaker, taintless pleader,
Unblotted lawyer, true proceeder;
Thou movest salvation even for alms,
Not with a bribed lawyer's palms.

And this is my eternal plea
To him that made heaven, earth and sea:
Seeing my flesh must die so soon,
And want a head to dine next noon,
Just at the stroke when my veins start and spread,
Set on my soul an everlasting head.
Then am I ready, like a palmer fit,
To tread those blest paths which before I writ.

WALTER DE LA MARE 1873–1956

THE LISTENERS

'Is there anybody there?' said the Traveller,
   Knocking on the moonlit door;
And his horse in the silence champed the grasses
   Of the forest's ferny floor:
And a bird flew up out of the turret,
   Above the Traveller's head:
And he smote upon the door again a second time;
   'Is there anybody there?' he said.
But no one descended to the Traveller;
   No head from the leaf-fringed sill
Leaned over and looked into his grey eyes,
   Where he stood perplexed and still.
But only a host of phantom listeners
   That dwelt in the lone house then
Stood listening in the quiet of the moonlight
   To that voice from the world of men:
Stood thronging the faint moonbeams on the dark stair,
   That goes down to the empty hall,
Hearkening in an air stirred and shaken
   By the lonely Traveller's call.
And he felt in his heart their strangeness,
   Their stillness answering his cry,
While his horse moved, cropping the dark turf,
   'Neath the starred and leafy sky;
For he suddenly smote on the door, even
   Louder, and lifted his head: –

'Tell them I came, and no one answered,
   That I kept my word,' he said.
Never the least stir made the listeners,
   Though every word he spake
Fell echoing through the shadowiness of the still house
   From the one man left awake:
Ay, they heard his foot upon the stirrup,
   And the sound of iron on stone,
And how the silence surged softly backward,
   When the plunging hoofs were gone.

W. H. AUDEN 1907–73

from A VOYAGE

I. WHITHER?

Where does this journey look which the watcher upon the quay,
Standing under his evil star, so bitterly envies,
As the mountains swim away with slow calm strokes
And the gulls abandon their vow? Does it promise a juster life?

Alone with his heart at last, does the fortunate traveller find
In the vague touch of a breeze, the fickle flash of a wave,
Proofs that somewhere exists, really, the Good Place,
Convincing as those that children find in stones and holes?

No, he discovers nothing: he does not want to arrive.
His journey is false, his unreal excitement really an illness
On a false island where the heart cannot act and will not suffer:
He condones his fever; he is weaker than he thought; his weakness
    is real.

But at moments, as when real dolphins with leap and panache
Cajole for recognition or, far away, a real island
Gets up to catch his eye, his trance is broken: he remembers
Times and places where he was well; he believes in joy,

That, maybe, his fever shall find a cure, the true journey an end
Where hearts meet and are really true, and crossed this ocean,
    that parts
Hearts which alter but is the same always, that goes
Everywhere, as truth and falsehood go, but cannot suffer.

R.S. THOMAS 1913–

THE BRIGHT FIELD

I have seen the sun break through
to illuminate a small field
for a while, and gone my way
and forgotten it. But that was the pearl
of great price, the one field that had
the treasure in it. I realize now
that I must give all that I have
to possess it. Life is not hurrying

on to a receding future, nor hankering after
an imagined past. It is the turning
aside like Moses to the miracle
of the lit bush, to a brightness
that seemed as transitory as your youth
once, but is the eternity that awaits you.

ALFRED, LORD TENNYSON 1809–92

CROSSING THE BAR

Sunset and evening star,
    And one clear call for me!
And may there be no moaning of the bar,
    When I put out to sea,

But such a tide as moving seems asleep,
    Too full for sound and foam,
When that which drew from out the boundless deep
    Turns again home.

Twilight and evening bell,
    And after that the dark!
And may there be no sadness of farewell,
    When I embark;

For though from out our bourne of Time and Place
    The flood may bear me far,
I hope to see my Pilot face to face
    When I have crossed the bar.

JOHN DONNE 1572–1631

HYMN TO GOD MY GOD, IN MY SICKNESS

Since I am coming to that holy room
    Where, with thy choir of saints for evermore,
I shall be made thy music; as I come
    I tune the instrument here at the door,
    And what I must do then, think here before.

Whilst my physicians by their love are grown
    Cosmographers, and I their map, who lie
Flat on this bed, that by them may be shown
    That this is my southwest discovery
    Per fretum febris, by these straits to die,

I joy, that in these straits, I see my West;
    For, though their currents yield return to none,
What shall my West hurt me? As West and East
    In all flat maps (and I am one) are one,
    So death doth touch the resurrection.

Is the Pacific Sea my home? Or are
    The Eastern riches? Is Jerusalem?
Anyan, and Màgellan, and Gìbraltar,
    All straits, and none but straits, are ways to them,
    Whether where Japhet dwelt, or Cham, or Shem.

We think that Paradise and Calvary,
    Christ's cross, and Adam's tree, stood in one place;
Look, Lord, and find both Adams met in me;
    As the first Adam's sweat surrounds my face,
    May the last Adam's blood my soul embrace.

So, in his purple wrapped, receive me, Lord;
    By these his thorns give me his other crown;
And, as to others' souls I preached Thy word,
    Be this my text, my sermon to mine own:
    Therefore that he may raise the Lord throws down.

EDWARD THOMAS 1878–1917

LIGHTS OUT

I have come to the borders of sleep,
The unfathomable deep
Forest where all must lose
Their way, however straight,
Or winding, soon or late;
They cannot choose.

Many a road and track
That, since the dawn's first crack,
Up to the forest brink,
Deceived the travellers,
Suddenly now blurs,
And in they sink.

Here love ends,
Despair, ambition ends;
All pleasure and all trouble,
Although most sweet or bitter,
Here ends in sleep that is sweeter
Than tasks most noble.

There is not any book
Or face of dearest look
That I would not turn from now
To go into the unknown
I must enter, and leave, alone,
I know not how.

The tall forest towers;
Its cloudy foliage lowers
Ahead, shelf above shelf;
Its silence I hear and obey
That I may lose my way
And myself.

DYLAN THOMAS 1914–53

DO NOT GO GENTLE INTO THAT GOOD NIGHT

Do not go gentle into that good night,
Old age should burn and rave at close of day;
Rage, rage against the dying of the light.

Though wise men at their end know dark is right,
Because their words had forked no lightning they
Do not go gentle into that good night.

Good men, the last wave by, crying how bright
Their frail deeds might have danced in a green bay,
Rage, rage against the dying of the light.

Wild men who caught and sang the sun in flight,
And learn, too late, they grieved it on its way,
Do not go gentle into that good night.

Grave men, near death, who see with blinding sight
Blind eyes could blaze like meteors and be gay,
Rage, rage against the dying of the light.

And you, my father, there on the sad height,
Curse, bless, me now with your fierce tears, I pray.
Do not go gentle into that good night.
Rage, rage against the dying of the light.

ACKNOWLEDGEMENTS

— ◇ —

The publishers would like to acknowledge the following for permission to reproduce copyright material. Every effort has been made to trace copyright holders but in a few cases this has proved impossible. The publishers would be interested to hear from any copyright holders not here acknowledged.

5. Carcanet Press for 'Leaving Belfast' from *The Pleasure Steamers* (1978) by Andrew Motion.
6, 8. Faber and Faber Ltd for 'A Removal from Terry Street' and 'Leaving Dundee' from *Selected Poems 1964–1983* by Douglas Dunn.
7. 'Poetry of Departures' by Philip Larkin is reprinted from *The Less Deceived* by permission of The Marvell Press, England and Australia.
9. Seren for 'Goodbye' from *Collected Poems* by Alun Lewis, published by Seren (1994).
20, 53. Faber and Faber Ltd for 'The Express' and 'The Landscape Near an Aerodrome' from *Collected Poems* by Stephen Spender.
21. Faber and Faber Ltd for 'The Whitsun Weddings' from *Collected Poems* by Philip Larkin.
24. 'Sassenachs' is from *Two's Company* by Jackie Kay (Blackie, 1992). Copyright © Jackie Kay. Reproduced by permission of Penguin Books.
26. The Society of Authors as the literary representative of the estate of John Masefield for 'Sea-Fever'.
27. 'The Mediterranean' is from *Collected Poems 1919–1976* by Allen Tate. Copyright © 1977 by Allen Tate. Reprinted by permission of Farrar, Straus & Giroux, LLC.
29. The James MacGibbon Estate for 'In My Dreams' by Stevie Smith.
30, 148. A.P. Watt on behalf of The National Trust for Places of Historic Interest or Natural Beauty for 'Mandalay' and 'The Way Through the Woods' from *Rudyard Kipling's Verse: Definitive Edition*.
32. This extract from 'Variations I: Travelling' is taken from *Michael Hamburger: Collected Poems 1941–1994* published by Anvil Press Poetry (1995).
35. 'High Flight' by John Gillespie Magee is reproduced by kind permission of This England Books.
40. A.P. Watt on behalf of The Royal Literary Fund for 'The Rolling English Road' from *The Collected Poems of G.K. Chesterton*.
41. Seren for 'The A40 Wolvercote Roundabout at Oxford' by John Powell Ward from *Poetry Wales* magazine.
43, 115. 'The Wiper' and part VI from 'Autumn Journal' are from *Collected Poems* by Louis MacNeice, published by Faber and Faber Ltd. Reprinted by permission of David Higham Associates.

45, 59. Faber and Faber Ltd for 'Night Drive' and 'The Peninsula' from *Opened Ground* by Seamus Heaney.

46. Alan Holden for 'Stopping Places' from *Selected Poems* by Molly Holden. Copyright © Alan Holden.

47, 61. The estate of Robert Frost for 'Stopping by Woods on a Snowy Evening' and 'The Road Not Taken' from *The Poetry of Robert Frost* edited by Edward Connery Lathem, published by Jonathan Cape. Copyright 1923, © 1969 by Henry Holt and Co., copyright 1951 by Robert Frost. Reprinted by permission of Henry Holt and Company, LLC, and Random House.

48, 65, 164. Faber and Faber Ltd for 'Night Mail', 'As I Walked Out One Evening' and 'I. Whither?' from 'A Voyage' from *Collected Poems* by W.H. Auden.

50. John Murray (Publishers) Ltd for 'The Metropolitan Railway' from *Collected Poems* by John Betjeman.

54, 133. Faber and Faber Ltd for 'On the Move' and 'A Map of the City' from *Selected Poems 1950–1975* by Thom Gunn.

60. Carcanet Press for 'The Journey' from *Collected Poems* by Charles Tomlinson, published by Oxford University Press (1985).

73, 162. The Literary Trustees of Walter de la Mare and the Society of Authors as their representative for 'Sea-Magic' and 'The Listeners' by Walter de la Mare.

74. Faber and Faber Ltd for 'Channel Crossing' from *Collected Poems* by Sylvia Plath.

76. Translation of 'The Seafarer' by Richard Hamer from *The Norton Anthology of Poetry*, 4th edition, edited by Margaret Ferguson and Mary Jo Salter, published by Norton (1996).

79. 'The Negro Speaks of Rivers' is from *Collected Poems* by Langston Hughes, published by Vintage US. Reprinted by permission of David Higham Associates.

88, 91. 'Wherever I Hang' and 'Out of Africa' are from *Lazy Thoughts of a Lazy Woman* by Grace Nichols, published by Virago Press.

89. 'Where the Scattering Began' is from *Penguin Modern Poets*, volume 8, edited by Jackie Kay, Merle Collins and Grace Nichols, published by Penguin (1986).

90. 'A Far Cry from Africa' from *Collected Poems 1948–1984* by Derek Walcott copyright © 1986 by Derek Walcott. Reprinted by permission of Farrar, Straus & Giroux, LLC and Faber and Faber Ltd.

99. From *The Arrivants: A New World Trilogy* (Oxford University Press, 1973). Copyright © 1957, 1968, 1969, 1973 by Edward Kamau Braithwaite.

103. Carcanet Press for 'Landfall in Unknown Seas' from *Early Days Yet* (1997) by Allen Curnow.

107. 'Columbus' by Ogden Nash is from *Candy is Dandy: The Best of Ogden Nash*, published by Andre Deutsch Ltd (1983).

108. 'Arrival at Santos' is from *The Complete Poems 1927–1979* by Elizabeth Bishop. Copyright © 1979, 1983 by Alice Helen Methfessel.

110. Rosica Colin Ltd for 'For a Journey' by Alan Brownjohn. Copyright © Alan Brownjohn 1970.

112. 'Home from Abroad' is from *Selected Poems* by Laurie Lee, published by Penguin. Reprinted by permission of the Peters Fraser & Dunlop Group Ltd.

113. Part 2 of 'Afterlives' from *Collected Poems* (1999) by Derek Mahon is reprinted by kind permission of the author and The Gallery Press.

114. Faber and Faber Ltd for 'On a Return from Egypt' from *The Complete Poems* by Keith Douglas.

119. 'Home Revisited' is from *Old Damson Face* by Bernard Gutteridge, published by London Magazine Editions.

120. '1. Down the M4' from 'Car Journeys' is from *Collected Poems 1948–1976* by Dannie Abse. Copyright © Dannie Abse 1977. Reproduced by permission of Sheil Land Associates.

121. 'Place of Birth' by Peter Hewett BA Hons (Oxon.) MA (OU) is reprinted by kind permission of James Hewett.

124, 128. A.P.Watt on behalf of Michael Yeats for 'Sailing to Byzantium' and 'The Lake Isle of Innisfree' from *The Collected Poems of W.B. Yeats*.

134. 'At the Tourist Center in Boston' is from *The Animals in That Country* by Margaret Atwood. Copyright © Oxford University Press, Canada.

136. Seren for 'Do you think we'll ever get to see Earth, sir?' from *Selected Poems* by Sheenagh Pugh, published by Seren (1990).

137. Robson Books for 'No Sense of Direction' from *Collected Poems 1950–93* by Vernon Scannell.

144. 'I. Bro' from 'Bloodlines' is from *Natural Causes* by Andrew Motion, published by Chatto & Windus. Reprinted by permission of the Peters Fraser & Dunlop Group Ltd.

146. 'Waiting for the Train to Start' by James Kirkup. To James Kirkup and the University of Salzburg Press, *Collected Shorter Poems of James Kirkup*, Vol. 1, OMENS OF DISASTER.

149, 169. 'Poem in October' and 'Do Not Go Gentle into That Good Night' are from *Collected Poems* by Dylan Thomas, published by J.M. Dent. Reprinted by permission of David Higham Associates.

156. Faber and Faber Ltd for 'Journey of the Magi' from *Collected Poems 1909–1962* by T.S. Eliot.

165. J.M. Dent for 'The Bright Field' from *Collected Poems 1945–1990* by R.S. Thomas, published by J.M. Dent & Sons.

INDEX OF POETS' NAMES

— ◇ —

INDEX OF FIRST LINES

— ◇ —